SKIING...
The Killy Way

by
Jean-Claude Killy

with
Doug Pfeiffer

Illustrations by Anthony Ravielli

Simon and Schuster · New York

First Printing

SBN 671-20977-9
Library of Congress Catalog Card Number: 74-156156
Designed by Edith Fowler
Manufactured in the United States of America

I would like to dedicate this book to
two men without whose constant help and
faith in me I would not have been able
to achieve the successes I have:
    To my father, Robert Killy
    and, to my good friend, Michel Arpin.

J.-C. K.

CONTENTS

6

INTRODUCTION

TAKE A GOOD LOOK at the photo on the facing page.

Sure it's Jean-Claude. It's also a revolution in ski technique. The picture was taken in 1966, and at that time very few skiers knew what the young, dynamic, wild-skiing Killy was up to. Today, however, most of the world's hottest shots are wise to what it was, and have since learned to make these fast jet christies.

Why a revolution? Well, for one thing, at a time when most racers were trying to "get forward," the charging Mr. Killy was trying to sit back. Just before the camera caught him in the pose at the left, he had brazenly put his weight on his heels, edged his skis and deliberately let them shoot into the air in front of him. And for another thing, his ski pole is planted well off to his low side. At the time, the technique experts droned the dogma that the pole had to be planted close to the ski tip. If Jean-Claude's style wasn't revolutionary it was out-of-sight heresy.

Need further evidence? Then note how he is anticipating his turn by leaning and twisting his upper body toward the center of the turn—just the opposite to what some coaches still preach about going forward and to the outside while reversing your shoulders. Defying dogma, the canny Killy first put his upper body where he wanted it, then swung his skis around to catch up. He had put together a more efficient way to make tight turns and get down the hill faster than anyone else.

Soon, alert racers and skiers turned a deaf ear to the theorists and coaches and, for a change, began to listen with their eyes. They saw

9

where ski technique was really at—right there where Jean-Claude's edges met the ice.

So? So Jean-Claude had developed a new, energy-conserving, time-saving way to get down through a flower garden of racing flags. And it left his competitors gasping at their sheepish reflections in all that silver hardware he collected.

So manufacturers were forced to come up with skis and boots which lent themselves to this new way of skiing. So, at long last, the hidebound traditionalists who controlled ski instruction had to open their eyes, ears, and minds to the fact that Jean-Claude Killy had something that ought to be looked into.

And he flabbergasted them all by saying, "Don't ski like me. Ski like you." An amazing guy, this Killy.

I first met him at the 1964 Olympic Winter Games held in Innsbruck, Austria, where I was a reporter/photographer, and Jean-Claude was doing his all for the French Alpine Ski Team. During those games, his performances weren't all that smashing—his best achievement was a fifth in giant slalom.

Ah, but what *pouvoir*—what potential! There was something about his forays through the gates that the French word *attaque* best describes. Sure, all elite class racers attack the course, but nobody did it by getting skis so consistently close to the key pole in each slalom combination. Killy's line of attack between the gates was so straight and so fast, however, that he constantly accelerated to the point where his speed finally exceeded that of his reflexes. Crash! It was plain. The day when Jean-Claude put it all together—speed, straight line, closeness—watch out, world!

Once during a *Skiing* Magazine interview, Jean-Claude said, "As long as my feet don't get over my head, I am not in trouble." Anyone who saw him race in those days can believe that. He was cat-fast; throw him in the air any which way, he'd always land feet first. And what reflexes! He moved faster than the swipe of an angry kitten's paw.

It wasn't only Jean-Claude's inordinate physical attributes and dedication that led him to his astounding victories—three Olympic gold medals, three times World Cup Champion, and the holder of countless other titles. On several occasions during the eight weeks of the Killy Challenge TV series (I did the "color" commentary), I became aware of Jean-Claude's uncanny ability to think in a crisis. The Killy Challenge consisted of two side-by-side slalom courses through which both competitors raced simultaneously. Killy's challenger left the starting gate with a carefully calculated handicap ranging anywhere from five tenths of a second to three seconds. But so carefully was Killy able to size up his competition that in many instances he allowed his challenger an even greater handicap. He'd leave the starting gate a few tenths of a second *after* he got his green light, and he still won.

On at least two other occasions he won through the exercise of conscious thought every bit as much as by his quick movements. Both instances were at the finish gate. In this kind of dual racing, the first man across the line wins. On the first occasion, when a scant few inches behind his challenger and just a few yards from the finish line, Jean-Claude took advantage of a small bump that had not been there at the time that he studied the course. Reaching the bump, he quickly launched himself into the air with such vigor that he put himself over the finish line first— by a hairbreadth.

On another occasion—a sudden death run to break a tie—he was involved in what in horse racing would have been a photo finish. But he had the presence of mind to shove his feet and knees forward, almost sitting on the backs of his skis as he did so, to break the electric eye beam, while his challenger (Pepi Stiegler) made the unfortunate mistake of lunging forward with his chest as if to break a finish-line tape. Tough for Pepi, for in skiing, it's getting both feet over the line first that counts.

Of such stuff and substance are champions made. As you read how Jean-Claude won his three Olympic gold medals, you'll learn more about that substance: dedication, determination, constant attention to detail, proper equipment, good coaching, and emotional support from someone you care about. I hope, as does Jean-Claude, that the wealth of information we've put together in this book will inspire you to become—if not a world champion skier—at least a safe and happy and much improved skier.

We suggest that you do not read this book as if it were a novel, but rather that you savor it with easy bites now and then, such as before going out to ski and just after a lesson, to reinforce what you've learned out on the slopes. It would not have been possible to put this work together without the help of several of the editors of *Skiing* Magazine—particularly John Henry Auran, Al Greenberg, and Cathie Judge. And of course, Tony Ravielli's drawings make it all come to life. Jean-Claude and I would like to thank them.

Good skiing—better skiing—to you all!

DOUG PFEIFFER

ABOVE: At age five or six, Jean-Claude sought thrills, not form.

LEFT: Jean-Claude at five—his first race. Could the heart-shaped *dossard* have signified love at first sight?

RIGHT: Jean-Claude thinking perhaps of a world outside Val d'Isère, but not concerned about the right way to hold his poles.

1 | MY FORMATIVE YEARS

I AM OFTEN ASKED, was there not one special moment when I decided to be a ski racer. No, it was more that a series of experiences throughout my early life cast the mold for me. Ski racing had to become my world.

For almost as long as I can remember I have loved to ski. I was just three when my family moved to Val d'Isère where my father was to start a ski club. It was 1946. I have few recollections of my birthplace, Saint-Cloud, a small town west of Paris. Our new life in the mountains made me happy right from the beginning. Skiing was as normal to the children of Val d'Isère as eating and drinking, and I played around on borrowed skis until I was five. Then finally I received a pair of my own, and from that moment on I was rarely seen without them. My parents nicknamed me Toutoune—I guess because I was like a crazy dog, obsessed with my skiing.

Val d'Isère was a very different place in those days. The roads were narrow and dangerous and there were only six hundred beds in the town (today there are eight thousand). Most of the buildings were rather rustic. I vividly recall one in particular because it concerns my early skiing. There was a roof covered by drifting snow. Smooth white drifts reached from the peak of the roof to the ground on one side and formed a perfect mountain for skiers my age and size.

When a *téléférique* was installed in town—Le Solaise—my

friends and I would always make one or two runs after school. In fact, I believe I did my first racing then because of a schoolteacher. He loved to ski also, so every Monday he'd take us out to the mountain, and one after another, we'd race each other down. Our equipment wasn't very fancy; in fact, I remember once my sister fell down and came out of her skis and boots! They went down the hill while she stood in the snow in stocking feet.

There weren't many instructors at Val in those days, and my friends and I devised an excellent technique for getting a free *Mont-Blanc*—a delicious dessert we loved made of cream, chestnuts and chantilly sauce. We would offer to teach the tourists to ski for the price of one cake, and generally we would end up with the cake, sometimes without having to give the lesson.

I skied as much as possible, making twelve or so long runs every day, yet I was only eight or nine. My father cautioned me that I was skiing too much, using up all my energy so that I had none left over to grow tall and strong. But, though I remained small for my size, I won my first victory about that time. It was for a slalom, and a cup was offered by Queen Juliana of Holland who was vacationing in Val d'Isère. Before the race, feeling very important, I went up to the race officials and demanded a *bossard*. How embarrassed I was when they laughed, and I found the right word for the racing bib I wanted was *dossard!* My first one, donned at the age of eight, was shaped like a heart.

My eighth year was also marked by my first ski trip to a race away from Val d'Isère. What an incredible discovery it was for me to find skiers on the other side of the mountain! In 1953, when I was ten, I won all three Alpine events in the Critérium des Jeunes, even beating the twelve- and thirteen-year-olds. For the first time my name made the regional papers, and this had a strange effect on me. I think that the competitive urge deep within me began to crystallize.

These were the sort of experiences that rooted me in skiing competition for good: seeing my name in the papers; having a special team sweater that not all my friends could have; going places they didn't go; and seeing how proud my parents were of me. There is a pleasant taste to victory, and soon I was thinking, Why not try for a bigger cup, a longer trip, a more important victory? Ski racing chose me—I was thrown into it as a way of life because it was all around me. And, because I discovered that I had a strong, competitive spirit, I stayed with it. I was a timid, secretive child, and not much of a scholar, so it was through skiing that I could express myself. How casual fate is in deciding who will make it, who won't. I skied with so many kids in Val, some that showed more promise than I, but none of them continued skiing. Somehow, I had the right circumstances and the passion to carry out what was started for me— the life of a ski champion.

At a young age I discovered I had the ability to imitate other skiers' styles. I have guarded this gift, for it served me well in developing my own technique, a do-it-yourself one, for I never took a lesson. I had great fun imitating French ski stars like Henri Oreiller, the first French Olympic champion. I learned a lot from him because he skied with a style years ahead of his time. Later, when I trained with the French team, I was especially influenced by the downhill form of Adrien Duvillard. He stayed low in the turns while the rest of the racers kept their bodies high. By watching many skiers and copying their styles, keeping some things, discarding others, I gradually developed a sense of what I wanted to achieve on skis—a style free of mannerisms, allowing for independent action of the legs, the lateral play of the knees and ankles controlling turns precisely and handling sudden checks and accelerations smoothly. I think most skiers lose the spontaneity they had as children. I didn't. I have kept loose on skis and trusted my own intuition, and though I made many mistakes along the way, my best-from-everything style worked magic for my last few racing years.

I have missed only two years of skiing in my life. When I was eleven I was sent to school at a place called Chambéry. Actually, in

15

LEFT: At three and one half—with borrowed warped skis.
CENTER: Jean-Claude at six. Shy to the world but proud of his equipment, the best then available.
RIGHT: Nine years old—frail and small for his age. Illness and separation from skiing awaited Jean-Claude in the near future.

those days this was only a three-hour drive from Val d'Isère, but to me it might have been the other end of the world. I couldn't understand why my parents would do such a thing to me, although later I learned it was because they were separating. I felt abandoned, robbed of the people and mountains I cherished, and I seemed very different from any of the children at the school.

I would look out through the dusty classroom windows and dream about Val d'Isère, my friends, the snow-covered mountains. I lost my appetite, had no interest in my studies. I became more and more unhappy and shut myself off completely from the people around me. I was still very short for my age as well as frail, and gradually my health became worse until I contracted a severe pulmonary infection. I was packed off immediately to a hospital at Saint Gervais and, during the four months there, I became more and more withdrawn. After I had partially recovered, the doctors forbade any skiing for at least a year so I was sent to a second school in Voiron, even farther away from the mountains. Here skiing was out of the question. Kept away from the sport which I loved and which represented freedom and happiness to me, I was miserable. I vowed to make up for lost time when I got out.

After these two school years, my next school was much closer to skiing. It was at Saint Jean de Maurienne. I was thirteen, and that summer I trained with the French B Team. Early in the school year, I was invited to compete in the Ilio Colli Cup at Cortina d'Ampezzo. Nothing could prevent me from going on that trip, so without the necessary permission from my school (which it would have been impossible to get) I headed for Italy with the team. The results? A broken leg and a dismissal from school! The world was at an end for me, I thought. But as he was often to do in the future, my father called me and said, "Don't worry Toutoune, I'm here." Our family was one of few words, but it was always a safe, good feeling to know that despite this, we were very close and warm. That broken leg of mine had another effect on me which underlines how I feel about the chances of fate. I was bedridden only a few months, but when I got up an amazing thing happened! I had grown fifteen centimeters (six inches). I believe all my growing years had been too active, as my father always said, so I had no time to grow. So breaking my leg, one of the most upsetting experiences in my life, in a way made my future victories possible. Now I had the size and strength to be a championship contender.

Within three months I was racing again—academia had lost out. In 1959 I won a number of victories including the Critérium des Jeunes. When I was fifteen I made the "hopefuls" for the French ski team, and in the winter of 1960 I trained with the team itself. I traveled and skied with them all—Adrien Duvillard, Guy Périllat, Charles Bozon, Michel Arpin, François Bonlieu. I was the youngest, and I listened and watched carefully to learn all I could.

The first international competition I won was a slalom, the Grand Prix de Morzine in 1961. I beat Léo Lacroix and Adrien Duvillard, who fell. That night I received the rooster, the emblem of the French team. The same week Guy Périllat, then only twenty-one, suddenly soared to international recognition with a series of incredible victories at Wengen and Kitzbühel.

My skiing at this time had a lot of punch and spontaneity. My mistake was in trying to sustain the straightest, fastest line throughout the course. This was to attain speed, but in the end I lost more time than I gained because of the terrible falls I took. In the slalom my attack was too strong, and I lost precision and control. Physically I wasn't able to handle the problems my great acceleration created. I hit the ruts, went out of control and lost my balance. But I was only seventeen. There was still time.

My excitement over the Morzine victory and my admittance to the French team were overshadowed by a terrible automobile accident a few days later. We skidded on a gravel section of the road and, while I came out with a few scratches, my friend and passenger was killed. It was a tragedy that matured me and affected me deeply. To pull myself out of deep depression I dedicated my life entirely to skiing, going at it with more force and determination than ever before.

The 1961-'62 season opened at Val d'Isère with the Critérium de la Première Neige. I fell in the slalom, and in the giant slalom I was given the number 39, which meant the course would be pretty rutted by the time I ran it. It looked as if luck was not with me that day, but I have never fought as hard as I did on that GS (giant slalom) course. It was worth it for I won, beating Adrien Duvillard and Michel Arpin by more than a second. The old order was changing—the newspapers heralded me as the future French ski champion. More important was my father's happiness and the reward he gave me—a chronometer he had had as a pilot during the war. I had always hoped to earn it.

In two months the World Championships at Chamonix were to be held and it was not clear who would be chosen to race. Perhaps it was fate, though I was pressing too hard for speed, but at the Ilio

Even at the age of five, Jean-Claude was the most properly attired and equipped of his racing companions. He's the one with the goggles.

Colli at Cortina I once again broke my leg. Soon after, the team for Chamonix was announced, and our coach, Honoré Bonnet, came to see me in the hospital with the news that he had intended to use me in the championships! I was terribly disappointed and, though I was at Chamonix, it was on crutches.

At this time I spent six months in the mountains of Algeria with the French army. By virtue of early leave I got out in the fall of 1963, but as soon as I reached home I came down with jaundice. That whole season, though I struggled through, I was never myself. My skiing had lost its punch and I was scrambling all the time to improve my point standing to qualify for the 1964 Olympics at Innsbruck. I accomplished this, and assured myself I could race among the first fifteen in all three events.

My performance at the Olympic Winter Games was a disaster: I placed fifth in giant slalom and I was eliminated in the slalom and the downhill. One of the problems: I had allowed an inexperienced technician to prepare my skis. I felt the time spent waxing was time wasted, and I had no talent for deciding which wax to use. I preferred to use that time studying the course or relaxing before the race. After Innsbruck, two ski men traveled with the team to take care of the equipment. Later Michel Arpin worked with me developing and caring for my equipment.

I was severely criticized for my performance at Innsbruck. A friend, noting my lack of strength, suggested a complete checkup as he thought I might not have recovered from my bout with jaundice. How right he was! I had been treated incorrectly and was suffering from amebic dysentery. So I again spent the first half of that summer recuperating, and then in August went to Portillo, Chile, to train for the 1964-65 season.

There was one race I'll never forget during 1965. It was at Kitzbühel. So far the French team had been thoroughly dominated by the Austrians, especially in downhill. We blamed our French-made equipment, but the manufacturers said we were just looking for excuses for our inability. Encouragingly, our downhill at Kitzbühel wasn't bad. Léo Lacroix placed fourth and I tenth. In the slalom the next day that indomitable Austrian, Karl Schranz, won the first run, ahead of everyone by 1.38 seconds. I wanted more than anything to give him a run for his money in the second run. I memorized the course thoroughly, studying the positions of the flags, the difficult spots, changes in snow conditions. Standing in the starting gate, I looked over to where Schranz was standing. He looked nervous, so I made an effort to look relaxed, flashing a confident smile his way. I was going to hit hard, to win. Skiing that slalom I found my style. All that I had been striving for actually happened—and worked! I didn't concentrate on the next gate, but on the fourth or fifth one ahead of me. This gave me time to anticipate the difficulties, to play with time. I was playing; I felt I could run through the course, my skis and I were so in tune. When I crossed the finish line, even the Austrians cheered, something they usually reserve for their own heroes. Schranz came in three seconds behind me. I won not just the slalom, but the combined, too. Only three French skiers had ever attained the same record at Kitzbühel before me. Moments like this make me forget the unhappy, bad times.

Two days later at the Megève downhill, I raced on Austrian skis and won. This proved to my country's equipment manufacturers that the French could win with the right skis. We became more determined than ever to catch up to and surpass the Austrians. That summer I went to Australia, racing and testing French skis with Léo Lacroix. We worked on fiberglass technology, an effort that eventually paid off for it was on the perfected model of a ski we developed that I won the World Championship downhill. Léo and I wanted a 230-centimeter downhill racing ski, longer than most skiers were using. We were sure it would work, but eventually we found out differently.

We also worked to improve our English that summer. I had come a long way from the narrow valley of Val d'Isère and now realized that an athlete, especially a skier, can become very closed off from life. I didn't want to forget about the realities of life, to become dependent on the French racing system—it's so easy to do. You have someone to make all the decisions for you; people are assigned to take care of both you and your equipment, and racing occupies you ten months of the year. When your racing days are over, you suddenly don't know what to do. I wished to avoid this sad situation.

When the 1966 season began I felt great. I had gained some weight and was stronger. My first race was a victory at Adelboden. The Lauberhorn was next, and I expected to place high, especially since I had the new long downhill skis I believed in. It was not to be, I was shattered. The long ski was a failure. Léo placed fifteenth; I was in the thirties! The team was attacked from all sides. Honoré Bonnet, our own coach, said we would never do well in downhill. The tension caused among us by his lack of confidence was in-

21

credible. But most of all we were angry. Léo Lacroix had given ten years of his life searching for one major victory. The team felt abandoned and it was not fair, since we were good skiers and fearless men, not the cowards Bonnet had pictured. We went on to prove him wrong. In the next few years I won many downhills, and Lacroix won that season as well. I never quite forgot that insult from Bonnet, even though I respect him greatly for creating a French team at the time he did. Although a champion makes himself a winner, he develops better in a close community with a team that has good spirit.

About this time, I learned a new, very beneficial method of relaxation—yoga. Georges Coulon taught me to understand it, and it left me relaxed and ready to fight in the French Championships at Courchevel. Although I left there without a win but with morale much improved, for Léo Lacroix had his downhill victory. Two events remained before the World Championships—I won the coveted diamond "K" in the Kandahar and the Giant Slalom title on the American circuit.

Portillo, 1966. I will never forget it. The French walked away with sixteen out of twenty-four medals! In the men's downhill I felt good. My skis were performing well, and Michel Arpin, my ever faithful friend, was in Portillo to care for them. An auto accident had kept him off the team and he was with us as a technical adviser. He had taken me under his wing and we worked together to perfect the team's skis. The day of the downhill was beautiful. I kept my line on the course—one different from anyone else's—and took the turns to the outside, keeping my style smooth. At the finish Arpin ran up to me. "You won," he shouted. "You're crazy!" I answered. "There are all the others still to come!" But it was true. Lacroix had second place. Most exciting, I was the world champion. THE CHAMPION OF THE WORLD! my mind shouted. Even two years later, winner of three Olympic gold medals, I didn't feel as happy, as elated, as I did at that moment.

Until he was nine, Jean-Claude seemed to take after his father, who was once a jumper on the French National Team.

For two nights after my victory, I didn't sleep a wink. When I lose, I sleep soundly, but it's always the same—when victorious, I relive the course a thousand times.

The Austrian press tried to minimize the French sweep at Portillo. They claimed the time of year was wrong, the altitude too great. My downhill was called insignificant because the run at Portillo was too short to count. They wanted to see me on a tougher course, and I was ready for them.

2 | MY VICTORIOUS YEARS

I BEGAN TO THINK seriously about winning at the 1968 Olympic Winter Games only after I won the World Cup in 1967. That victory was terribly important for me because it gave me tremendous confidence and assured me I could win in all three disciplines—giant slalom, slalom, and especially downhill, my weakest event. That 1966 F.I.S. World Championship in Portillo, Chile, was the beginning, and the continued victories I put together in 1967 proved to me that I could do it.

During the many major races that counted toward the 1967 World Cup, many journalists and friends talked to me about the forthcoming Olympics, wondering if I could do what Toni Sailer had done in 1956—win all three gold medals. I put such questions aside at the time because I wanted to concentrate on getting a perfect score in the season-long events for the World Cup. I knew later on there would be time to think of the Olympics.

Preparation is everything to winning. It is easy to say, "I am going to win," but it is hard to convince yourself that it's really possible. After all the other racers are thinking the same thing. So I don't think about it; instead I concentrate on my training and my

RIGHT: Even when launched into the air at 60 to 80 mph , Jean-Claude tried to hold his tuck. The event here is the downhill, in which he won his first gold medal at Grenoble, 1968.

24

72- 9231

equipment, which really determine who will make it. Then, on the day of the race, whether it is an Olympic contest or not, I can say with confidence, "I am ready."

I think I had a slight advantage over the others in preparing for the Olympics because they were the only challenge left to me in ski racing. I'd dream about winning, think how fantastic it would be, but never did I tell myself I would win. However, I did decide not to try for the combined title at Grenoble, partly because the medal for it is an F.I.S. one, not an Olympic one, and partly because that's what I did at Portillo. After I won the downhill, I didn't ski as hard as I could have in the other races just to make sure I wouldn't fall. I was a disappointment to myself.

When I returned home in the late spring of 1967 after the World Cup, I did a little car racing because I enjoyed the excitement, but mostly I trained to keep in condition. I'd ride my bicycle up the Col de l'Iseran, a steep pass outside Val d'Isère, going as fast as I could both up and downhill. Going downhill fast on a bike is something like downhill racing, and is very good for the nerves.

In July, Michel Arpin came up with many pairs of skis for me to try out. There were skis with a great variety of flexes and bases, some for hard snow and ice, some for soft snow—skis for everything that might happen at Grenoble. It was at that time we decided that I would use 220-centimeter downhill skis. The longer ones we'd experimented with hadn't been so good for me and also I knew the downhill at Grenoble would be won in the turns—nine important ones—and shorter skis would be easier to turn. Michel and I worked for four days high in the mountains that July. He clocked me on every run and kept a chart on how well I did on every pair of skis in all kinds of snow conditions. Then we picked the ten best pair and Michel went back to the factory to try to make even better ones.

Michel has always skied with much the same style as I do, and we used the same size skis and boots. He had always known that I didn't like to prepare skis—mounting bindings, filing edges and waxing—although my loss at Innsbruck had convinced me of its importance. So from the Portillo races, Michel took care of everything concerning my skis. All I had to do was race. It was fabulous. We understood each other perfectly. When everybody was up in the morning preparing their skis for the race or for practice, I could stay in bed and sleep a couple of hours longer because I knew Michel would do a good job on my equipment.

He did more than take care of my skis. In addition he acted like a coach, timing me and the other racers during practice and during the races. And he was always picking up information that would be useful to me. Besides that, Michel was great fun and relaxing for me to be with.

At Christmas time 1967, Michel once again came to Val d'Isère with another load of skis. By that time we had had the first big race of the season, the Critérium de la Première Neige in Val d'Isère. I won one of the two giant slaloms, but the downhill was cancelled due to lack of snow. It was very odd, but when we tested the new skis here that Michel had brought, the ones we picked in July still remained the best.

My results in the big January races were disappointing. I had good runs and beat one of the top Swiss, Edi Bruggmann, in the Adelboden giant slalom, but I couldn't really get anything going. I think I was trying too many things. Every day, new skis. And the weather was very bad. That may have thrown me off a bit. It was a good thing I didn't have to prove anything in those races. Even though I wasn't winning very much, I never lost my confidence. But I must admit, when you don't win and don't win, you start to think. And this is not good. When you think too much, you become conscious of what you are doing and you get into trouble. You must be spontaneous—like a cat, just move fast, without thinking.

At Kitzbühel, the last big race before the Olympics, I got off my line in the downhill—a bad mistake—and yet I came in second. It was unbelievable. I said to myself, "Without that mistake you would have been the winner for sure. So now you are back in tune and you should be okay for Grenoble."

27

Another important thing happened at Kitzbühel. Toni Sailer told me how he won his three Olympic gold medals at Cortina d'Ampezzo. He said what helped him most was staying off skis for several days just before the Olympics. "You have to relax and not try too hard," he told me, and I could believe him because I knew he always was a great sportsman. He didn't try to press me, or really encourage me. The way he gave me that hint was in a very matter-of-fact way, and I decided to follow his advice.

The next week was the last race before the Games. It was at Megève. I went up the mountain for the slalom, then decided I didn't want to race. It was the first time in my life that I ever did that. I told Bonnet that I wanted to go away for a few days and not ski.

"That's all right," he said. "Do what you want. I'm sure you know what's right for you."

Within an hour I was on my way (I had my car with me) and I went to the home of Louis Jauffret at Montgenèvre in France's southern Alps where there is always sun. It was a relief to do nothing but lie on the sundeck, just relaxing, after all the bad weather we had in the races before the Olympics. Louis was really fantastic to me, hiding his disappointment over not qualifying for the team in slalom. "That's okay, I don't care," he said, "But I care for you and I want to put you in a good mood to win." I told him I didn't want to think about skiing at all, and that's what happened. While I was at his house, for over a week, we didn't talk skiing once.

I rejoined the team when the Olympic courses opened for training. Michel had arrived before me and had everything ready. I decided to concentrate completely on the downhill because it was the first and most difficult of the races. I knew if I did well in it I would do well in slalom and giant slalom.

It felt good to get back on skis again after my rest, but on the first day of training my times were quite slow. Michel was timing me against the other racers, but he told me not to worry. Sure enough, by the second day I was as good as everybody else, and by the third, I was really becoming the master of the course. My times over the important sections were much faster than those of the others. This was psychologically important. I began to feel very confident. Bit by bit, all my little concerns began to drop away so that the only thing I had to do was to go to the starting gate and run the course.

Michel was tremendous in getting me into this mood. He kept coming up with bits of information that put my mind at ease. He would scout around in the training rooms and the nightclubs to get intelligence on wax and equipment and then he would study his graphs of the times so that we knew exactly how we stood. One day he heard that Gerhard Nenning, who had won the downhills at Wengen and Kitzbühel and was one of my big rivals, had trouble with his skis and was trying to find a new pair. This was good for me because I knew I had prepared better than he had and also when you don't have the right skis before a race you start to worry, especially if it's the race of your life, as it was for him. Even before the nonstop training run, I reached the point where I knew I was in the best physical condition possible, my equipment was ready, and I knew every inch of the *piste* by heart. There was nothing else I could do except relax and wait for the day of the race.

But it wasn't going to be as easy as all that. I felt right on the morning of the downhill, but I made a mistake. I always take a run of a mile or so before each race so that my wax is adjusted to the snow conditions. To do this at Grenoble I went to a slope I thought had powder snow on it. But the wind had blown off the snow, and all that was left was scratchy ice. By the time I got to the bottom, I had practically no wax left, and when I got back to the starting hut, there was no time left to rewax.

I met Michel at the start and told him what had happened. I said, "I think I am going to lose the race." Funny, but I didn't feel panicky. All I could think was, "Too bad I will not win because of an unlucky accident."

But Michel remained very confident.

"That's okay," he said. "There is no problem. I've been down the course and you will win without wax. Just get a good start."

I always concentrate on a good start and push very hard out of the starting gate. But in the Olympic downhill, when the starter said, "*Allez,*" I don't think I ever pushed so hard in my life. *Formidable!* I shot out of the gate and picked up lots of speed in the first section of the course. By the second gate I felt very, very fast—fast enough to win. So I completely forgot about the wax and concentrated on the course, particularly the two bumps at Col de la Balme. Everything had to be timed just right if I was going to land high on the second bump—necessary if I were to be able to carry plenty of speed across the flat. The last part of the course was quite rutted by the time I came through—the winner by eight hundredths of a second. Unbelievable! I am sure I won the race at the top, by the time I had reached the second gate.

There was a tremendous excitement at the finish line, and I can't remember all that happened. When everything quieted down I asked Michel, "Were you really sure about my winning without the wax?"

"Not at all," he said, laughing very hard. "But up top I didn't think was the place to tell you that."

After I had won that downhill gold medal, I did begin to think seriously about the other two golds. The giant slalom was the next race, and I knew it was my best event. I said to myself, "This is the week for me. Nobody can stop me."

And nobody did. My winning the gold medal in giant slalom looked very easy to everybody because I won the race by over two seconds, but there were some important reasons for it. First of all I had not practiced giant slalom since I had won it at Adelboden, so when I started training again at Grenoble I was fresh and eager. More important was a belief I held about two-run giant slaloms, which by the way, I am not in favor of. I've always raced the two runs as two separate races. For the first run at the Olympics, it was a beautiful, sunny day and the course was hard and almost icy. I went all out in the first run, attacking each gate very aggressively as though there were no tomorrow. I think the other racers were holding back a bit, trying to save something for the next day. Well, the next day was very foggy and the *piste* had softened during the night, and the chances of anyone catching up with me by making a fantastic run went out of the window. All I had to do was run the course smoothly. I didn't have to risk anything. Billy Kidd made a beautiful run under these bad conditions and managed to beat me, but he was so far behind from the first run that he couldn't make up the difference. This was a very unlucky Olympics for him.

It was an easy victory, but I was still happy about it. After the close call in the downhill, it was good to be way out in front. I felt I had great momentum, great confidence, and, as it turned out, I needed it in the slalom.

The slalom turned out to be a long, drawn-out race and very controversial. Since I was in the center of those controversies, I can give you only my version of what went on.

There was only one gold medal at stake, but actually we racers had to run three races for a chance to win it. First there was the elimination race. The skiers raced in groups of six, with half of each group being eliminated and the other half advancing to the classification race to determine the starting order for the final slalom. I believed these races were terribly unfair, but I went along with the elimination slalom. Then when I realized that I had to race again only to establish my starting number, I was very bitter. I made up a petition to the F.I.S., (Fédération Internationale de Ski) asking that the classification race be cancelled. Nearly all the first-group racers signed it and I presented it to Marc Hodler, president of the F.I.S. "I am sure you are right," he said, "but the race was approved by the F.I.S. and it is too late to change anything." But he did assure me that if the weather were bad and if there were danger to the racers, the jury would consider cancelling the race. This is what happened when the fog didn't lift. I never at any time threatened to strike, but some of the racers may have felt that way about the

31

classification race. I am sure they wouldn't have done it though, even if the race had been run.

Of course, the next day the weather was just as bad, perhaps worse. I thought it stupid to hold the slalom under those conditions, but I didn't think the jury could do anything about it. The Xth Winter Olympic Games were to come to an end after this Sunday, and if the slalom had been postponed it would have created a big mess in Grenoble.

With the weather the way it was it was a very difficult course. Most of the time I couldn't see more than a gate in front of me as I was climbing up for the first run. I had No. 15, ordinarily not good, but this time it was a help because, as I got into the starting gate, the fog lifted a little bit so I could see the gates. I thought that a sign, a good omen.

I made a good run, a very strong run under the conditions, and it gave me a half-second lead over the strongest field ever to race in the Olympics. Fourteen racers were within less than a second of my time, and most of them closer than that. But it didn't bother me to have the lead. Some racers get nervous when they are out in front, but I don't. I think it is good to have a lead because the others have to press very hard to catch up, and, when one presses, it is easy to make a mistake.

For the second run, the fog was solid. I tried very hard to make another fast run. I'm sure I could have done better if the weather had been clear, but under the circumstances I felt pretty good. Still, there was a chance for someone to beat me if he took wild risks.

When Haakon Mjoen of Norway came down, he was more than a second faster and beat my combined time, but I wasn't worried. I felt it was possible for someone to be faster than I, but not by that much. Sure enough, the word came down that he had missed some gates and was disqualified.

Karl Schranz was something else again. His time for the first run was closer to mine than Mjoen's, and he had beaten my second run by a little more than half a second.

Nevertheless, I had a feeling that everything would turn out all right. My brother was with me and he was very anxious to know what was going on. I told him, "There was some trouble on top. Just wait and don't make any comments. It could be that he was disqualified." But then I added for insurance, "Maybe not. Maybe he is the Olympic champion." But I didn't really think so.

It was funny that day seeing Schranz. He had a big, wide smile as he posed for photographers, but it wasn't an Olympic smile. He wasn't smiling with his eyes, and I felt he was acting. I am sure he knew the jury was not going to recognize his claim that he missed the gates because of interference.

When, after a long meeting, the jury disqualified Schranz and named me the winner, I was very, very happy. The three gold medals were an impossible dream come true. I was only sorry that there would always be a question about my medal in slalom, at least in the minds of some people.

But that's ski racing. There's no way of telling exactly why you win or why you lose. There are a lot of little things that make a difference: Your mood, the weather, the courses, your equipment, and maybe what you eat. For me, the rest I got with Louis Jauffret beforehand, and the help I got from Michel Arpin were the secret weapons that played a big role in my Olympic victories.

Immediately after the Games, of course, I felt something of a letdown. For some time Mark McCormack, an American who had helped golfers like Arnold Palmer and Jack Nicklaus earn more than a million dollars each, was urging me to consider the possibility of coming to America to capitalize on my fame. But I did not feel quite ready to give up ski racing. Since the events at the Olympics counted toward the World Cup, and I already had a clear-cut point advantage toward winning this trophy, I decided to continue racing for the balance of the 1968 season. After all, I could always decide to turn professional later, couldn't I? And my name would be even more important, I thought, if I were to win the World Cup for a second consecutive year.

ABOVE: Karl Schranz at the finish of his controversial slalom run in the 1968 Olympics "didn't seem to have a real victory smile."
OPPOSITE: Jean-Claude also skied slalom with the more conventional reversed-shoulder technique. He made this gate, but not without knocking down the pole.

The next two months of racing passed slowly for me. My concentration was not entirely on racing. However, I did manage to insure that I would win the World Cup again. Much of the time I was thinking of my future. I had neglected school in my passion for skiing, I was not trained for business or trade, and I didn't want to become a guide or a ski instructor.

At the end of the season I decided to follow Mark McCormack's advice—and ever since I have been busier than ever making ski movies, doing "The Killy Challenge" for TV, doing personal appearances, helping design skis and boots, consulting with editors, and of course making money and seeing the world. I only hope that you who follow in my tracks will have as much success as I, and make as many real friends along the way as I have. Good luck!

34

3 | EQUIPMENT AND CLOTHING

It's AMAZING how ski equipment has been simplified in the last ten years. All skiers, not just racers, used to have to wax their skis every day, even several times a day in the springtime. And what a chore it used to be to break in a pair of lace boots. I knew many a racer who would put on his new, custom-fitted competition boots and stand in a tub of warm water for a few minutes until the leather was thoroughly soaked. Then he'd lace the boots up tight, forcing the leather to shape to the bumps and hollows of his feet as it dried. Even with all these precautions, many racers (and skiers) developed painful bone spurs where the boots rubbed sensitive spots. Those spurs sometimes had to be removed by surgery.

But such pains and chores have now been removed from the sport. Plastic has come to the ski world. Now skis have plastic bottoms (usually polyethylene of some sort) that slide reasonably well on all surfaces. With boots, plastic was first used for soles, and, as a result, you had no more worries about boots curling up to interfere with binding release. Then plastic was used to make hard outer shells that are marvelously waterproof and easy to maintain—at last, no more nightly polishing! And now there's foam fitting—a system that lets you have a boot custom-molded to fit your foot in minutes, right in your ski shop! A mixture of chemicals that produces polyurethane foam is injected or poured into the boot shell directly or into a bladder that fits inside it. You put your foot in, and *presto!* The

foam flows around every nook and cranny, perfectly contouring your foot. After ten minutes or so, you take out your foot and let the plastic cure for half a day at the most, and there you are with perfect-fit boots.

But just because I say that ski equipment has been simplified, I don't mean it is simple to buy what's right for you. Not yet. In fact, the dazzling array of brightly colored, shiny skis, boots, and poles in the ski shop can really be confusing. You could buy skis to co-ordinate with your new parka, or buy the boots your favorite racer uses, but I don't advise doing either. I've learned a few things about choosing equipment that I'd like to pass along. But putting yourself in the hands of a well-trained salesman in a good specialty ski shop is one of the first things to do.

Buying Skis

You know, the first thing I would tell you about finding the right ski is to be honest with yourself. Consider how well you ski, how often, and sincerely, how good a skier you think you want to become. Also—how tall are you? How much do you weigh? Are you in good physical condition? How many days did you ski last year and how many do you anticipate skiing this year? What kind of terrain and snow do you usually ski on? Powder? Ice? The steep, narrow trails of the East or the wide-open spaces of the Rockies? Have you got what it takes (including desire) to become an expert? The answers to these questions will direct you to the right ski.

Wood skis are the cheapest, and, if you are a beginner, you can learn on them. However, they have a short performance peak and must be carefully cared for to last more than a season. Metal skis, on the other hand, almost take care of themselves. They have a long life expectancy and, for this reason, have the best guarantees. I find that metal skis are easy to turn and ski well in soft snow. Expect to pay between $90 and $180 for a popular, recreational-type metal. Another type of ski, the F.R.P., or fiberglass-reinforced plastic, is favored by most of today's hotshot skiers. I used this type during my racing career, and still find it a high performer. F.R.P. skis, like finely tuned racing cars, are lively and capable of ready response. If you like to carve your turns or jet your christies, these would be the skis for you. The price range is the same as for metal skis, although a few brands sell for as much as $250. And then there's metal/glass combination. If you are a better-than-average recreational skier who can afford a $180-and-up price tag, this ski could be for you. It has the longevity of metal combined with most of the high-performance characteristics of fiberglass.

Buying Boots

You'll want a boot that buckles, and, most likely, a plastic one. But again, I'll repeat, the most important thing is to find a boot that fits you and your brand of skiing perfectly. Boots are the most important piece of equipment you have. During the racing season, I needed a new pair every six weeks! If you are content with an easy stem christie and ski only a few weekends a season, too much boot can be as bad for you as too little. What I mean is a boot that's too stiff and has been designed for high-speed, mogul-bashing *avalement* or jet-christie skiing will make it difficult, if not impossible, for you to ski the way you want to. On the other hand, as it's likely you'll want to ski the modern way (see pages 152-153), the right boot will make it possible. It must have the locked hinge, high back, raised-heel features. The locked hinge, by physically locking or stiffening the junction of the shaft and the foot allows you to have immediate control over either the fronts or the backs of the skis. The raised heel puts your knees forward so you can sit back without losing your balance, and the ultra-high backs provide extra support for muscles not quite strong enough to maintain this position and also act as a springboard from which you can bound forward when you need to. The resulting control, however, is so direct and immediate that it is very easy to overcontrol your skis.

Spend as much as you need to get the right boots. It is false economy to save a few dollars. For casual skiing, $60 will bring you a serviceable boot. If you ski several weeks a year, spend between $60 and $100 to get a boot that will last several seasons. If you need a heavy-duty boot, one suited to hotdogging recreational skiers, expect to pay $100 to $175. Go to a shop with depth in its boot stock —one which is experienced with on-the-spot foaming methods.

Buying Bindings

Of the almost one hundred bindings on the market, only about a dozen can be considered good buys in terms of reducing the risk of injury to your legs. Be sure that the one you purchase fulfills the following criteria:

1. *Compatibility of toe and heel.* It is best to buy toe-and-heel units matched by the manufacturer. Unless you know what you are doing (and sometimes the salesman waiting on you has no more knowledge than you), mixing is a risky, even disastrous, practice.

2. *Anti-shock characteristics.* This is the ability of a binding to move off center under a momentary load, and then return to center when the load is removed.

3. *Low inherent friction.* This prevents freezing of the pivot points when high load (your boots) are applied.

4. *Consistent releases (left, right, and vertically).*

5. *Consistent contact.* The contact between boot and binding should remain unchanged despite wear and use.

6. *Easy-to-adjust units and adjustments that are self-locking.*

7. *Ease of entry and exit.*

8. *A good runaway device that does not interfere with the release function.*

9. *Low maintenance.* Whatever is required should be easy to perform.

10. *Operation immune to freezing.*

11. *Compatibility with the boots you will be using.*

Some of these points you can check yourself; others need the assistance of a ski-shop specialist.

Buying Poles
and Other Hardware

Further on (page 51), you'll find a pointer on choosing the right length pole. I'd like to add here you can buy inexpensive poles for about six or seven dollars, but chances are they will be made of soft aluminum which will bend out of shape very easily. Generally the more you pay for poles, the better quality you will receive. Ask your retailer about guarantees. Also, test poles before buying for swing weight. That means when you grasp the pole correctly, swing it back and forth as if skiing. You'll usually find the more expensive models swing easily and quickly and are more responsive than less costly ones. These qualities are important if you want to become a good skier.

Other items you'll want to consider—rubber clips to hold the skis together; boot trees to make it easy to store or carry your ski boots; ski bags and boot bags for easy traveling with your equipment; sunglasses and storm goggles—the latter a must for foul-weather skiing; a touch-up edge sharpener; a waxing kit; and, possibly, a small knapsack or fanny pack. Many accessories are available to make your ski days more pleasurable. Investigate them for yourself—a larger catalog would be necessary for me to list them all here.

Buying Clothing

Ski clothing should keep you warm but not overly warm. They must allow you to move freely because ours is an active sport, and they must be durable. After these conditions are met you can pick from the wide variety of colors, styles, and looks that make skiers such a colorful lot.

Dress in layers—several light layers will keep you warmer than one or two heavy ones. If you find you are too warm, you can shed a thin layer; too cold, add another one underneath.

Let's be specific. On your feet you need a thin cotton or woolen sock and over it, a thick woolen one—unless you are luck enough to have the new foamed boots. Then you may find that just one pair of light woolen socks is enough. For your legs, long underwear under your ski pants not only keeps you warm but adds a little padding to make falling softer! And you *will* fall—all skiers do. With your ski pants you should wear a turtleneck, and an undershirt, or a long-underwear top beneath. Some skiers like the fishnet type of undershirt; others prefer a conventional cotton or cotton-wool blend.

Next, wear a light- or medium-weight woolen sweater, then a parka. Be sure that the parka is made specially for skiing. There are "ski looks" on the market which don't have the durability and freedom of movement that a real parka must have. A supplement that is hardy is a nylon windshirt. In warm weather, you can wear it over a sweater with no parka. If it's very cold, the windshirt makes an extra windproof layer under your parka.

Pants? You have a choice. The classic look for skiing, stretch pants, are made of a fabric that combines wool, nylon, and Spandex

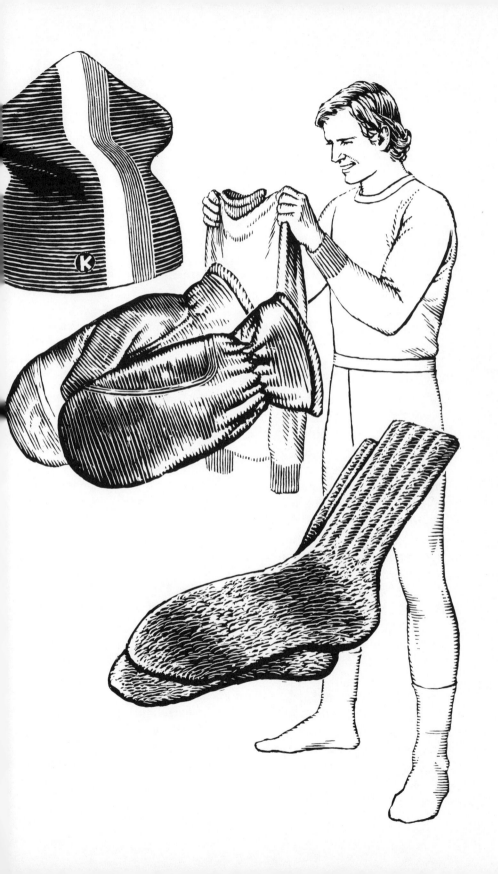

in varying proportions—usually the higher the percentage of wool, the higher the price. These pants are practical, warm, comfortable, and smart-looking. A number of styles are available in stretch pants —the most popular has outer legs that go outside your boots like regular slacks, and inner legs with a stirrup that goes inside the boot to keep the pants in place. Stretch pants cost between $35 and $90.

In the past few years another kind of pants—the warm-up— have really caught on with skiers. When I raced, these were the kind of pants we would wear over our skinny, lightweight racing suits to keep warm before the race. When a racer was ready to go, he'd just zip off the pants and step into the gate. That is where I think the fad for warm-ups started, but they've come a long way. You can get the bulky-looking, very warm ones—they are most popular in bright colors, prints and stripes. Underneath these, wear regular stretch pants, jeans, or just underwear, depending on the weather. Now there are close-fitted nylon pants that are variations of warm-ups, but are meant to be worn by themselves, without stretch pants underneath. These often come in ciré (a soft, shiny nylon) and, to look like a European skier, wear a pair with a matching parka. I know many people think stretch pants are the sexiest outfit a girl can wear, but when I see some of the girls in Val d'Isère in their bright red-and-yellow ciré outfits, I'm not so sure they're right! For warm-up pants, you'll pay between eighteen and fifty dollars.

Body heat is lost quickly through a bare head, so a hat is a must to keep all of you warm, not just your head and ears. Knit hats, like the one I have on in the photograph, are practical and come in a variety of styles and colors. Fur and fake-fur toques and helmet styles are also popular. Any hat you wear should be designed so it can come down over your ears when necessary. While the hood on your parka is good protection against wind, wet, and long, chilly chairlift rides, on its own it does not provide enough protection.

44

On your hands, you'll need special ski mittens or gloves. They are usually made of specially treated leather and are snug around the wrist to keep snow out. Mittens are warmer than gloves, so if your hands get cold easily you may prefer them. Many skiers wear gloves because they want the flexibility of separate finger movement. Ski mittens or gloves are usually lined with foam or other insulating materials. Color and style are up to you—gloves no longer come in black only.

Now you are suited up for skiing from head to toe. One last word—it's very important to be dressed right for the temperature. If you are too warm and sweat too much, your clothes will become damp and lose their insulating properties. As soon as you stop moving, you can get thoroughly chilled because of those uncomfortable, damp clothes. If you aren't dressed warmly enough, you've got trouble, too. Cold muscles don't react well, and you are more apt to fall. In addition, if you take a bad fall when you are cold, your joints and muscles are stiffer and therefore more prone to strains and sprains. So keep warm *mes amis*.

In the balance of this chapter you will find an assortment of helpful pointers—things I consider especially important in the selection of your equipment.

A

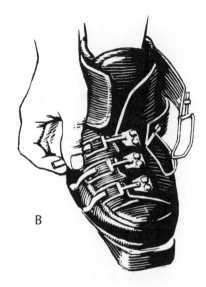

B

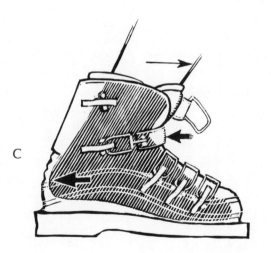

C

Boots —
Perfect Fit Is a Must

Like all good skiers, I believe your boots are the most important part of your equipment. Good ones can even coax satisfactory performance from what Americans call "lousy skis."

Boots must be comfortable—otherwise you'll suffer all day and never enjoy skiing or learn it well. By comfortable, I don't mean soft like a *pantoufle* (bedroom slipper), but they should fit snugly, hugging the contours of your foot like a glove. Sometimes what feels like a fit problem with buckle boots is just a matter of not having them fastened correctly. Here's how to achieve maximum control and comfortable fit:

When you first put your foot into the boot, push it forward till your toes touch the end (A). You should barely be able to insert your fingers between your heel and the back of the boot. That's so when your heel is properly seated in the back of the boot, you will have some room up front in which to wiggle the toes. Next, starting at the front, buckle each buckle on the loosest possible setting until the fourth one is reached (B). Third, close the fourth buckle at moderate tension, flex your ankle to force the heel back, then reset its tension again, and repeat (C). If you can raise your heel inside the boot the boot is too big. Be sure to get one that holds down your heel snugly. It must not move up and down or from side to side if you are to get full performance from your skis.

What Ski Length for You?

Just about every expert has his own opinion about the proper length of skis, and I am no exception. Here I'll try to give you enough guidance so that you can make your own decision. From the illustration you can see what I mean by a long ski. The shortest ski shown is just that—short, your own height. The intermediate length shown is about right for most people.

For your first few times on the snow almost any ski will do. Maximum length should be only six inches taller than you, and, in fact, if the ski barely reaches to your chin, you'll find learning easier. There are even ski schools that start adults off on skis as short as four feet, and this is a good idea. For beginners, then, or for people who are not particularly athletic, I think a ski which is only an inch or two higher than the top of the head is best. This length provides all the stability necessary for not-too-fast skiing, and it turns easier than a long ski. I do think that habitual use of skis shorter than your height should be done only with the supervision of your instructor, or by persons who haven't the opportunity to get into good-enough shape to enjoy the sport of skiing to its utmost.

If you are an intermediate skier, then choose a ski three, six, nine, or even twelve inches taller than your height. Choose the shorter options if you are either short, lightweight, not expertly coordinated, or not in great shape. Choose the longer lengths if the opposite characteristics apply to you.

If you are an expert, you can use long skis—twelve, fifteen or even eighteen inches greater than your height, and from your years of experience, you will know which is right for you.

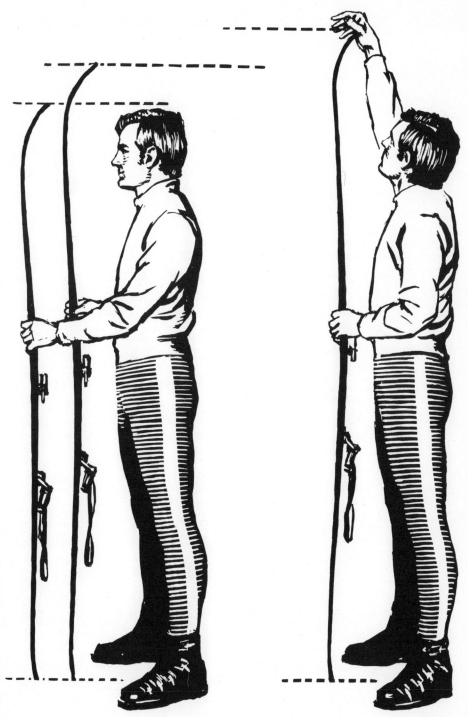

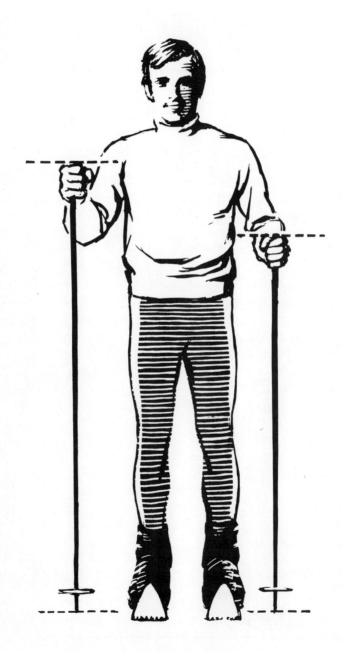

The Right-Length Pole

Some great racers I know like to use long poles, that is, ones that reach to the armpit or higher. But give me a short pole—one that reaches to just above my waist, with the tip not stuck into the snow, when I am standing on my skis. I need the quick maneuverability I get from this length. What's right for you? Most likely, not anything proportionately more than an inch or two shorter than mine, and perhaps something proportionately a couple of inches longer. To put it another way, a pole that's about 75 per cent of your height is average; for the modern techniques such as *avalement,* one about 66 per cent is more suitable.

If you are unsure, why not buy a pair of poles that are on the long side and have them cut down an inch at a time by your ski shop until you find a length you like? Your skiing will improve when you discover the pole length you like.

What Bending Flex
Means to You

For most skiers, a very important matter in the choice of skis is bending flex. Only experience will teach you what flex you like, and here are some tips on how you can feel it out in a pair of skis.

In the illustration I am stressing a ski to test its flex. In the large picture my hand—the one grasping the ski's waist—is pushing at right angles to the ski to feel how much resiliency the ski has. In the small illustration I am stressing the shovel area to see how stiff the ski's tip is. Each type of ski has its characteristic feel, and you will learn as you become a more experienced skier, to feel out the one that is right for you. Unless you are very heavy or especially strong and athletic, do not choose a ski which is too stiff. To do so is to court unpleasant skiing. Another way to get a feeling for the stiffness or flexibility of a pair of skis is to stand them up bottom to bottom. If you cannot take all of the arch (camber) out of them by squeezing *with one hand* and causing the bottoms to touch along their entire running-surface length, then chances are the ski is too stiff for you.

Where to Mount
Your Bindings

It seems to me that many recreational skiers know very little about where exactly to mount bindings on a new pair of skis. It does make a difference, believe me. If the bindings are too far forward or too far back, your skis won't behave properly, no matter what you do.

If you are going to mount bindings on your skis yourself, here's what you ought to know. I take for granted you know they go on top. Next, your goal is to place the binding so that the center of the ball of your foot will be over the center of the running surface of the ski. You can see the location of this point in the illustration.

Here is a good simple method for finding the proper placement point on your skis: (1) Measure, as shown in the illustration, the straight-line distance from the tip back to the tail of the ski. (2) Divide this distance by two and mark the point on the ski. You'll now have the point where the front edge of your ski boot should touch the ski. Mount the toepiece of your binding so that it will hold the boot in this position.

This formula should be modified if the sole of your boot extends out more than a quarter of an inch beyond the toe of your boot, or if your boot fits so that your toe rests far back from the toe of the boot. In either case you'll have to mount the bindings slightly ahead of the point marked on the skis to compensate.

This formula is, by and large, what most specialty ski shops use, and I can recommend it to you. But, sometimes, I have had to move bindings forward or back a little to get them placed just right for me. Racers alter the formula to fit their special needs. For slalom,

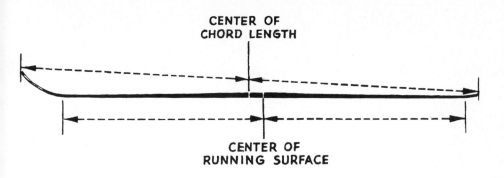

CENTER OF
CHORD LENGTH

CENTER OF
RUNNING SURFACE

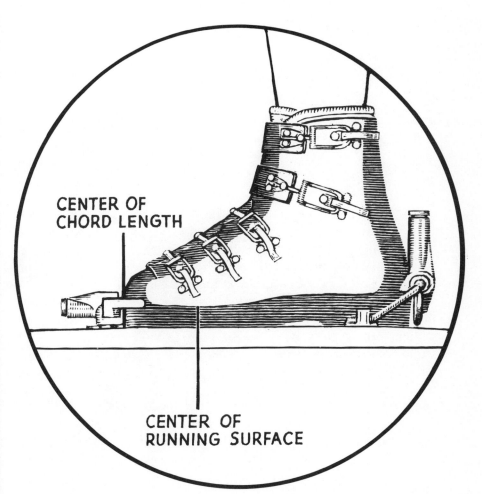

CENTER OF
CHORD LENGTH

CENTER OF
RUNNING SURFACE

the binding would be placed about a half inch in front of the mid-point, and for downhill racing, back from the midpoint about a half inch.

Understanding
Binding Release

There's no excuse for anyone to ski without reliable release bindings—there are so many good ones available. But don't call these safety bindings because they are not necessarily safe. If they are not adjusted properly, they can release inadvertently, when you don't expect them to, and you can be hurt. I learned early in my skiing days to check my bindings regularly and closely. I have even had the misfortune to be unable to finish a race because my bindings released when they shouldn't have. Tremendous twisting forces are involved in making a fast, precise slalom turn. In the illustration you see how my whole body is beginning to twist to my left—that's called anticipation—while my skis are still turning to the right. If my bindings weren't adjusted properly I could twist out of them, fall, and at the very least, lose the race!

Train yourself to check your bindings regularly—ideally every time you put on your skis, or at least before each day of skiing. Check each ski for equal right and left release. If the toepiece of your binding is mounted at an angle and is off by as little as one-sixteenth of an inch, or if the notches on your boot are not cut equally deep, the bindings will not release equally to left or to right. You'll come out too easily on one side and, thinking they are set too loose, you'll tighten up on the adjustment screw. This may make release to the other side impossible. You're then in for trouble! Coming out of a binding when you don't want to can be almost as dangerous. Do yourself a favor—have your bindings checked by the simple machine (Lipe Release Check) carried by most serious ski equipment shops. Don't take chances!

Equipment Organizer

When you have gone to all the trouble of getting to a ski area, you want to be sure you haven't forgotten to bring something that you'll need. It's easy to forget something like ski gloves or boots in the last minute rush to get off. So why not make up a checklist of things you'll need. Or use my checklist as a guide.

As you see, my list is in three sections: *Musts* which you will need on any trip—day, weekend, or longer. *Handy* are those items which are good to have but not essential. *Extras* are the things which you may or may not want, depending on where you are staying, how long, and what you plan to do. Some of these "extra" items would include those things you'd want to consider when you are taking a ski vacation of a few days or more.

Before you go on your first trip of the season, check off the items you already have, and then you'll know what you'll need to buy. It will help avoid those last-minute lapses of memory.

MUSTS

- Skis
- Poles
- Wax
- Parka
- Sweater
- Turtleneck shirt
- Hat or headband
- Goggles or glasses with yellow and green lenses
- Lip and sun cream
- Boots on boot tree
- Ski lock
- Ski ties or carrier
- Stretch pants
- Thermal underwear
- Socks—heavy, light
- Mittens or gloves
- After-ski boots
- Binding tool, silicone spray
- Tissues, Band-Aids, aspirin, sewing kit

HANDY

- Additional sweaters
- Lightweight parka
- Warm-up suit, pants
- Fanny pack, belt pouch
- Camera, film
- Foam padding for boots
- Nylon windshirt
- Skier's release check
- Extra stretch pants
- After-ski sweater or T-neck
- Knickers, knee socks
- Face mask
- Additional underwear, socks, T-necks, glove liners
- Edge file, base repair kit

EXTRAS

- Pajamas, robe, slippers
- Extra apparel
- Pants suit, culottes, long skirt for girls
- Flannel slacks, blazer or sport jacket, silk T-necks for men
- Dress shoes
- Dress-up *après*-ski boots
- Jacket, coat, cape
- Gloves
- Handbag or ski pouch
- Tie or ascot

4 | FUNDAMENTALS—
THE NEOPHYTE
AND NOVICE

WHEN I SKI I'm full of *joie de vivre,* as you can see in the accompanying illustration where I am doing a jet christie. Someday it will be easy for you to do a high-spirited turn like this one. Maybe it will take you a few years, but no matter. An amazing thing about skiing is that you can have fun from your first day. You'll enjoy learning, and as you learn you'll gradually take on bigger challenges. Even such fundamentals as walking, climbing, falling, and getting up carry with them a certain sense of accomplishment. I wish it were possible for me to take you out personally the first few times to make sure you don't give up. But since I can't, I must urge you to seek the help of a good ski school. A wise instructor will have you practice on flat terrain for about an hour before taking you to ride up a lift or ski down even the gentlest slopes. That way you get used to the length and weight of your skis and you don't feel incompetent and frightened.

Without proper guidance, your first few hours on skis may leave you frustrated, overworked, overtired and discouraged—perhaps even to the point of abandoning the sport. I'd hate to have that happen because I know how satisfying skiing can be for everyone.

So, after an hour or so of overcoming your initial awkwardness, you'll start sliding downhill, and the exhilaration of speed will be added to your sense of accomplishment. Then you'll need to know how to change your direction.

Another amazing thing about skiing is that it keeps getting

61

more exciting the more you learn. It's as if every new maneuver mastered unlocks the door to a whole new roomful of thrills. The traditional ski-school maneuvers you'll learn are these: schussing, traversing, sideslipping, the snowplow stop, the snowplow turn, and the stem christie, all of which are included in this chapter. I hope that you'll not be like all-too-many skiers who think they have reached the ultimate when they know how to do stem christies. These turns are just another step along the way to where the great joys of skiing actually begin—the parallel christies, which are dealt with in the following chapter.

How long will it take before you learn to ski? Some of you may learn the maneuvers in this chapter after only four or five days on skis. Others may take two or three weeks, or the better part of a season of weekend-only skiing, since skiing is more than just maneuvers. It takes a lot of experience to develop the balance, confidence, and muscles to be a really good skier, and I'll tell you how to get this experience in a future chapter.

Some Special Words
for First-Timers

If there's a specialty ski shop near you, go there—not necessarily to buy, but to look at the equipment and clothing. Ask a few questions. Don't be pressured to buy until you've a good idea as to what you'll actually need. Since boots are the most important piece of equipment, take a special look at the different prices, before deciding on a pair. You can also find out names of ski areas you might like to visit, and the directions for getting to them. The shop will have ski-area brochures and maps as well as skiing magazines and books. Get information about local clubs and bus tours to local areas. I would give serious consideration to joining an organized group, using rental equipment for your first two or three outings, maybe for your first season.

Whether or not you go with an organized tour, don't forget lessons. Once at the area, go to the information booth and find out where and when classes meet, and what kind of lift ticket you should buy. A two-hour class lesson costs from $2 to $5; private instruction $8 to $15 per hour. A lift or tow ticket costs between $4 and $10. For most of you, a class lesson is best the first few times you ski.

Once you enroll in a class, if you do not already have your equipment, go to the rental shop and get fitted for boots, skis, and poles. If you have no special ski clothes yet, wear something warm that you can move around in. Don't overdress—you won't be going up high yet, and learning to move with your skis on snow creates plenty of natural warmth. (See pages 42-45 for clothing information.) Your instructor will help you get skis and bindings on right. Make sure to have your bindings checked for proper releasing before

64

leaving the rental shop. Once in class, watch and listen carefully to what the instructor is saying and, if you don't understand, say so.

I stress ski school even though I never took lessons myself. But you must remember that when I started, I was very young. I skied almost every day, and I had some of the world's best skiers—like Henri Oreiller—around to help me. It was different for me. Most people progress faster with greater safety if they are in class. The risk of injury in skiing is small anyway, but it's the least for ski schoolers. Even if you have friends who are willing and anxious to teach you, I think you are better off with a pro. It's hard for even the most well-meaning friends to remember the questions and troubles they had as beginners. Also, in their eagerness to have you improve quickly, they are apt to encourage you to try slopes beyond your ability. The risks of injury are not worth the excitement—it is better to learn the right way, right from the start, and leave the thrills of fast downhill skiing until you've developed the right muscles and skills to virtually eliminate the chances of getting hurt.

In this chapter you'll find advice I would try to convey to you if I were right there by your side as you are learning. Read carefully before you go to the slopes, and again after a day or two of skiing, to reinforce what you've learned on the snow.

When to Take
a Lesson

I told you in the introduction to this chapter how important I think it is to start out by taking lessons. I'd like to reinforce that. As you get better, you may find that skiing is so much fun, so absorbing, you become complacent about your progress. It amazes me to look at a slope of weekend skiers and see how much bad skiing goes on. There are two ways to learn the techniques for different or unusual snow conditions. The first, and hardest to learn, is to watch better skiers than yourself and try to imitate their movements. The other way is to take a lesson from a certified ski instructor. If he is good, you will learn a number of very helpful things, even in just one lesson. So, when you have reached a plateau in learning, my advice is to take a lesson—better yet, take four or five. If you've developed a peculiar or special problem which can best be corrected through several hours of concentrated effort, your instructor will recommend a private lesson. In the illustration you see me leading down a couple of people who want to improve. I have instructed them to stay very close to me and to follow as exactly in my tracks as they can. This way they can imitate my movements, almost without thinking of them, and profit by my ability to choose the right (easiest) place to turn. An accomplished instructor will ask you to do just the same both in class and in private lessons. Do your best to follow closely when your turn comes.

In the United States most ski schools are divided into the following six categories: *Class A*—First-time Beginners; *Class B*—Snowplow; *Class C*—Snowplow Turn; *Class D*—Stem Turn; *Class E*—Sideslip, Beginning Parallel; *Class F*—Parallel Christies.

In addition to these categories, some ski schools also offer special instruction in advanced maneuvers, deep snow skiing, and slalom, giant slalom, and downhill racing.

Get the Proper Grip
on Your Poles

Very early in my racing career I lost a race because of the careless way in which I gripped my poles. I had allowed my leather straps to stretch so much that when the tip of my pole held to the snow more than I expected it to, the pole was wrenched free of my hand. You can believe that ever since then I have been sure to check that my straps fit tightly, that they are short enough to fit as snugly to my hand as my hand fits to my glove.

Every instructor knows how important it is for novice skiers to hold their poles properly. When they don't, the fingers have to squeeze the grip, and this tenses up the arm and makes all movements stiff. I know that if an advanced skier does not have a good grip on his poles, he can't rely on their support during the critical moment that occurs every time he makes a sharp, fast turn. Here's how to grip your poles correctly:

1. If the strap is leather, give the smooth side a half twist inward so that the loop formed will rest smooth and flat around the glove. Some poles have plastic straps, pre-twisted to conform to your grip. Always slip your hand, including the thumb, through the loop made by the strap by passing it up from underneath.

2. Pull back on the strap so it rests against the back of your hand.

3. Grasp the pole with your thumb on one side, fingers on the other. Both parts of the strap should now rest between your hand and the pole.

4. Now press down on the strap to take up any slack. The top

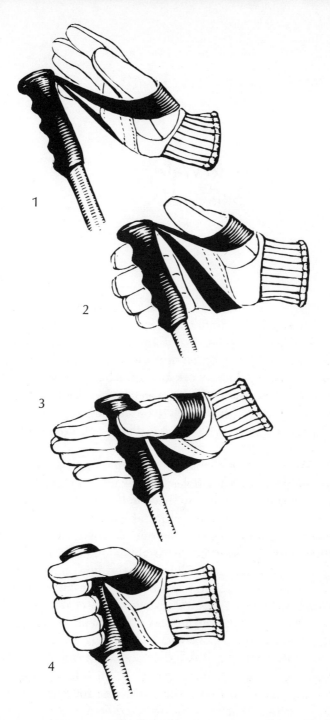

of your hand with the glove on should now rest no more than a quarter inch from the top of the pole. If more of the pole protrudes above the top of your hand, then the strap should be shortened.

How to Walk
on Skis

Here's how to take your first steps on skis. Even if you have already skied, you might spot something to improve upon.

I can tell a great deal about a skier's ability just by watching him walk along a flat area of snow. If he is stiff like a tin soldier and if he is making hard work out of what should be an easy gliding walk, then I know that he doesn't feel at home on his skis. Walking on level snow with your skis on should be easier and faster than walking on snow without them. If it's not, you are doing something wrong.

To start, pick a smooth, flat place to practice. Now try to walk without planting your poles in the snow so that you can concentrate on what you are doing with your legs and skis. Let the poles trail behind. Feet should be comfortably apart—six to eight inches. Skis should be parallel. Now slide one ski forward in your first step and follow with the other in a natural walking rhythm. Don't pick up the ski to move it forward. Slide it ahead with a thrusting movement.

In the illustration I am bending the knee of my forward leg as I am walking—I'm not stiff-legged. Also, notice where I am looking: My head is up and my eyes are ahead—I am not looking down at my feet and skis. As you walk, focus on something in front of you. Most beginners take short, small steps—*don't*. Slide your forward foot in a nice long glide. If the illustration were a motion picture, you'd see that I slide with the forward foot, push off with the back one. Then, as the forward foot loses momentum, it stops on the snow and becomes the pushing foot as the other foot slides forward. Notice my upper body is inclined forward a little to keep my momentum going.

After you feel that you are going well without the aid of your poles, start using them to help you push forward and aid balance. Place the pole in the snow opposite the leading foot and behind its heel, as you see in the illustration. The pole should be on an angle, slanting backward from your hand. The placement and angle allow me to push with my arm, shoulder, and back—if the pole were planted further forward and vertical, I'd have to pull on it and that doesn't work. As you push off with the pole, your back leg comes up to take over the leading position and you plant the other pole in the same manner. The movement is a natural one—it's the same arm and leg alternation you use on "dry land."

The Kick Turn

In France we call the kick turn *une conversion*. Experienced skiers do it without a thought, but even Olympic champions had to cautiously try it for the first time way back when. It's a snappy maneuver: You stand facing one way—zip, zap—you're facing the opposite direction. When you first learn it, you should do it a few times just for fun.

More than fun, it is very useful to know when you are climbing a slope diagonally using a half sidestep (page 75). When you reach the side of the slope, you do a kick turn and continue diagonally upward in the opposite direction. It is also useful in getting you down a slope that's over your head—one that is steep, with conditions that prevent you from doing a moving turn. Take a slow traverse over to the side of the slope; stop; do a kick turn; traverse to the other side, kick-turn again, and so on. You'll get down safely.

Here's how to do it: Stand with your skis heading across the hill, neither up nor down. Make sure you have a steady platform before you start. In the illustration, I'm going to kick with my left foot

1   2

3

4

(dark shading). This is the downhill ski. In picture 1, I have all my weight on my right foot while sliding the kicking foot back and forth a bit to get the feel of the movement. Do the same, and, when you have mastered the balance, start your kick with a little backward windup (picture 2). Kick up the whole leg, waist high. At the same time, bend your foot back a bit (the opposite of pointing your toe) so that the tail of the ski comes to rest on the snow well forward, by the tip of the other ski. If you don't get it up that far you can't do the rest of the turn properly. Now, using the tail of the ski as a pivot point, flop the tip of the ski out to the side and down flat next to the other ski, as you see me doing in pictures 3 and 4. I have my ski pole on that side, out of the way, behind me, and my body is turned halfway. *Voilà!* You'll be in what ballet dancers call "fifth position."

Complete the turn by putting your weight on the kicking foot while bringing the other one around—don't get it caught on that pole behind you. It helps to keep the feet and legs close as you bring around the ski. Your body and the right-hand ski pole turn the rest of the way, along with the turning skis (picture 5). When you finish up, you'll be facing the other way, as in 6. Practice a few times—it will become easy for you.

5

6

Climbing:
The Sidestep

You should know how to climb up a hill with skis. Lifts can get you to the top, but sometimes you have to climb to the lift. Also, climbing is good practice for learning to feel at home on skis and for developing the muscles in your legs and ankles—vital for the turning maneuvers you will do.

One way to climb with skis is called the sidestep. It's like stepping sideways up the stairs. Facing crosswise to the hill, with your feet together and skis parallel, lift the uphill ski, then move it sideways and slam it into the hill. Then you stand on this ski and slam the downhill ski up next to it. Repeat this and you'll find yourself moving right up the hill, skis sideways. If the snow is icy or hard, you may have to slam your skis quite hard as you move them. This makes the steel edges bite into the snow so your skis won't slip out from under you as you take your next step—like walking sideways on the sides of your feet. The downhill pole is the most important. Plant it next to your downhill foot with your hand next to your hip so you can push off from it as you climb. Keep the uphill pole out of the way of your ski as you move it sideways up the hill.

There is a practical variation of this maneuver, called the diagonal- or half sidestep: Walk forward as you sidestep with your uphill ski. You will then be going up the hill diagonally. This is easier than going straight up—it's half walking and half climbing.

Climbing:
The Herringbone

Another way to climb with skis is called the herringbone, so-called because of the track it makes in the snow (*see illustration*). It is strenuous, but it gets you straight up the hill fast. You face directly up the hill with your skis in a V-position, the point of the "V" behind you. First lift one foot, then the other, walking on the inside edge of each ski—sort of knock-kneed. Note how I hold my poles—the grip of each is butted into the bottom of each palm. As I push from it, the lower pole and my arm form a straight line. Feet and arms move opposite one another, just as in regular walking. It's important to note that my poles are never poked in the snow ahead of my feet. To do so would be to try to pull myself up rather than push myself. For the same reason, my hands stay behind my hips.

Climbing up a hill is a good way to get the kinks out before the first run of the day or after a cold chairlift ride. It speeds the circulation and loosens up your muscles. Try it—the extra bit of limbering up could save you from ending up with a torn muscle.

How to Schuss

For me there's a real challenge, a special thrill, in going straight down a ski slope. You don't make any turns—you just go all out in a sort of power dive. Skiers call this *schussing*—a German word, which, appropriately enough, means to shoot.

Of course schussing can be dangerous, but only for the reckless person who seeks the thrills of speed, but who is unable to control either his speed or his direction. For those who go about it with care and consideration, schussing gives rewards of improved skills, greater confidence, and thrills.

For me schussing is easiest and safest when I keep my feet and skis apart about the same width as my hips. When I go really fast— over 45 miles per hour—I don't try to ski with perfect form, for I am too busy concentrating on balance and keeping my weight distributed evenly on each foot. When you schuss, you too should be aware of these things. Also keep your ankles, knees, and waist loose so they can bend and unbend constantly, compensating for changes in the terrain.

As a beginner, learn to schuss on very gentle slopes, even if you go no faster than 5 miles per hour. Look for obstacle-free slopes which have a flat runout so you can come to a natural stop. Stand on your skis as I do in the illustration. Intermediates should seek out a similar slope, pitched, of course, at a steeper angle.

To become an advanced skier or an expert, you must develop the confidence and ability to ski fast. An excellent place to practice fast skiing (after you master the basic maneuvers in this chapter) is at the bottom of a steep slope. First, practice schussing the last ten

to twenty yards. Then, gradually work your way into starting higher and higher up the slope. Your enjoyment will increase enormously as you learn to savor the taste of more speed in your skiing. As you lose your fear of speed, you'll find that your mind and muscles become more relaxed. Consequently you will be capable of making turns at high speed. And what a thrill that will be!

How to Fall Safely

I've said it before, even I fall. The important thing is to fall properly so you avoid injury. Let me show you how.

Start by sitting back on your skis as though you were going to sit down on a chair, as you see me doing in the first drawing of this sequence. However, don't sit down all the way or you'll be taken for a toboggan ride. Keep your hands up and your poles pointed rearward—if a pole is pointing in front of you, the tip may catch in the snow and your hand and the pole may be forced back to bump you in the head or face.

At the last split second, as you are sitting down, move your *derrière* off to the side and sit down on the snow. (*See second and third illustrations.*) Because most of your weight will now be on your seat, you can keep your skis parallel and their tips free of the snow to avoid their catching and digging in. The same goes for your knees —keep them up and free of the snow or one might dig in and turn your graceful little fall into an "egg beater," a dangerous rolling tumble.

If you are heading across a hill when you do your fall, sit down on the uphill side of your skis and you'll have far less a distance to fall.

Really practice this falling exercise—it does wonders for your confidence.

FALL LINE

How to Get Up
After a Fall

If you are in good shape, getting up after a fall is no big deal. If you're not, it's not so easy, and if you are in really bad shape, sometimes it's impossible. Sprawl on the floor and then try to get to your feet. Complicate the situation by trying to get up with skis on your feet and poles in your hands to get an idea of how hard it can be. On the snow it's even worse because your skis slip back and forth. But practice and know-how will conquer. Here's the easiest way to get up after a fall:

First, make sure your skis are below you. Then place them across the slope so they are perpendicular to the fall line. With your skis across the slope they won't take off down the hill—forwards or backwards—when you get back up on them.

Now get your feet underneath your hips so that your weight is directly over your feet as you get up. Next, place your ski poles side by side in the snow next to your uphill hip. Hold them together with your uphill hand down by the baskets and the other hand holding the ends of the grips, as I show in the illustration.

Now, as you push up with the aid of your poles, roll yourself back over your skis. It's very important to keep your hips ahead of your heels at all times when you are striving to get up. Once you are again vertically situated over your skis, move your lower hand up the poles as you regain an upright stance. Then stand up and catch your breath.

FALL LINE

The Importance
of the Fall Line

When you are a *débutant* to skiing, you may think the fall line has something to do with the place you fall. In a way it does, but the relationship is only coincidental. The fall line is actually an idea —a handy way for skiers to describe their orientation on a slope. Put another way, the fall line is the imaginary path which a ball would follow if it were allowed to roll slowly downhill. In French we call this line *la ligne de la plus grande pente*—the line of the greatest pitch. It could also be called the line of least resistance or of fastest descent.

This illustration shows how I am about to ski into the fall line. Since I'm making a turn, no sooner will I ski into the fall line then I will ski back from it to complete the turn. Skiing straight down the fall line is called *schussing*; skiing across it is called *traversing*. If you ski straight down, making wigglelike turns, you are said to be skiing close to the fall line.

It is important to recognize this line for several reasons: One, if you want to slow down, you must turn away from the fall line, into the hill. Another, if you want to gain speed, you turn downhill or into the fall line. Also, when you understand what the phrase means, communication with fellow skiers and instructors will be easier.

Oh, I almost forgot—the relationship of the fall line to the place where you fall. Whenever you turn toward the fall line you will pick up speed, so you'll feel a moment of anxiety; sit back on your skis as they slide faster and faster, and finally fall. Where? On the fall line!

FALL LINE

Traversing

Traversing is simply a matter of skiing across a hill or across the fall line. As a learning skier, it is one of the first and best ways you have to control speed. You can pick any angle at which to ski across the hill, so you can go at any speed you want. In fact, when your skis are at right angles to the fall line, you won't even move. Point yourself downhill a few degrees, and you'll traverse at a slow, comfortable pace.

There is a proper way to stand on your skis for traversing. It's important to learn for your future parallel-christie skiing, so you might as well learn to do it early.

Take a good look at this illustration. I am traversing a steep slope with the hill to my left and the valley to my right. Notice that the uphill edges of my skis are cutting a firm platform, which makes them go in the direction they point. One of the basic principles of good skiing is to keep body movements and positions symmetrical—the same on both sides. Because of the hill, note that my left foot is higher than my right. As far as that goes, everything on my left is similarly higher. A line drawn between my toes would be parallel to a line drawn through my knees, hips and shoulders. This position is called *angulation*. By rolling my knees and ankles toward or away from the mountain, I can make my skis edge more or less depending on the grip that I feel I need for ice or soft snow and for the pitch of the slope.

Sometimes, as I push my knees toward the slope, I tip my shoulders slightly downhill. This helps me to keep slightly more weight on my lower ski. On hard snow, that's an advantage when it comes to holding my traversing direction.

The Snowplow—
The Action to Take to Brake

I don't make a habit of snowplowing. It slows you down and that's the last thing a racer would want. The snowplow is a braking maneuver. In the illustration, you see me standing directly over my skis as if I were sliding straight down the fall line. The extra legs superimposed on the figure show the tails of my skis pushed out into the classic snowplow V-position with the tips no more than a few inches apart and the skis resting on their inside edges. Note that my body is properly centered over both skis to keep my weight distributed equally on each one.

To learn the snowplow, first practice on the flat where there is no possibility of sliding forward or backward. Place your skis—one at a time—in the snowplow position and then back in the schussing position. Now hop on both skis into the snowplow position and then hop back into the schussing position. Many ski instructors would prefer that you not learn to snowplow until you already know how to traverse and sideslip, but this isn't always practical. At some ski areas, it's best to know how to stop very early in the game! Forewarned is forearmed, however—practicing the snowplow too long can cause you to develop a habit which may take years to get rid of. How long is too long? Maybe a half hour, or a day or two. It's an individual matter and only a good instructor can advise you. In any case, the moment to stop is when your first reaction to the slightest concern for your welfare is to snowplow, rather than to sideslip or turn.

The snowplow has some redeeming values. You learn independent leg action. You develop muscles to control your skis. You

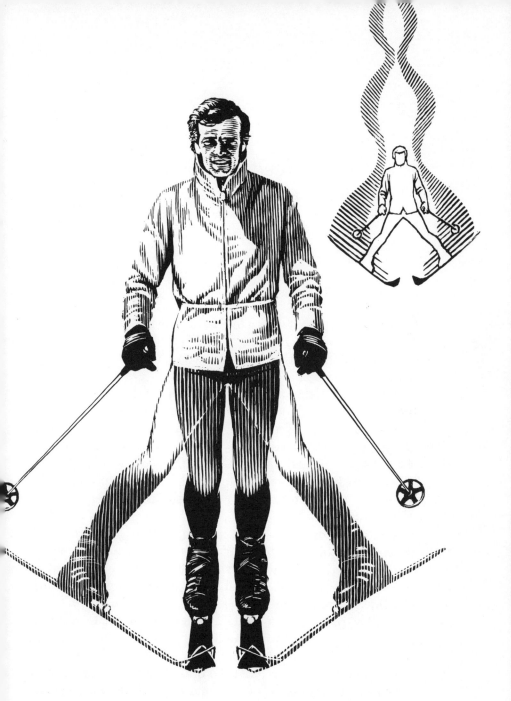

learn edge control. And you learn to come to a stop. The small diagram shows a valuable snowplow exercise. Ski straight down a gentle slope alternately pushing your heels apart and letting them come together.

Control Speed
with Turning Radius

In skiing the name of the game is turning. Sure, it's a thrill to head your skis down the fall line and go all out, but you can't and won't want to do that all the time. Turn you must.

We turn to avoid obstacles and to follow a certain path or trail down the slope. But this is only part of it. Too few skiers realize that turning is the chief means of controlling speed—you can go faster or slower merely by changing direction. If you want to slow down or stop, you turn toward the hill, or, as instructors say, turn away from the fall line. If you want to gain speed, you head down the hill or toward the fall line. And, when you want to maintain a constant speed, you keep turning, alternately toward the hill, then toward the valley.

In the illustration, you see me turning with two purposes; one, with the intention of going fast, and the other of keeping a rein on my speed. The straight arrow marks the fall line (straight down) of this slope. In the left figure, I am about to turn toward the fall line (to my right). Since my intention is to ski rather fast, I won't turn much, and the snaky line to my left shows the course I will take. That's called skiing close to the fall line.

In the other figure my intention is to go slower, so I ski back and forth across the hill more, and the dotted lines show the slower course I will take. My turns are now more complete and rounded, and they take me farther away from the fall line (more into the hill) before I head back toward it. In this way I check my speed.

I believe many skiers hold back their progress by not thinking how they should use turns to control speed. Unfortunately, many

beginning and intermediate skiers get into the habit of stemming for control, even if they are capable of doing parallel christies. If you are in this group, I hope you now see that you don't need that stem —you can get all the control you need by the amount you turn.

The Snowplow Turn

Here is a demonstration of a "neutral" way of making linked snowplow turns. The sequence starts from the snowplow position. Note that I keep my body comfortably centered between the skis, that my weight rests almost flat-footed along the entire sole of each foot, and that I bend forward slightly at the waist to maintain balance. Now follow me down the hill. I begin to turn by pushing both knees forward and in toward the center of my intended turn—that's to my right. If the slope isn't too steep, my skis will turn to the right. As I begin to turn off the fall line, my weight gradually transfers automatically to my left ski (the one on the outside of the turn). I can increase the turning rate by leaning over that ski, thereby adding weight to it, and by increasing the bite of its inside edge.

To turn to the left I push both knees forward and in toward the imaginary center of a turn to the left. This gradually brings me into the fall line—and immediately back from it, if I keep up the twisting action. As before, I can speed up the rate of the turn by leaning out over my outside ski—after it has begun to point toward the new direction—while simultaneously pushing my outside knee forward and toward the inside of the turn.

Almost all ski-instruction experts agree that every skier must learn to snowplow at some early stage (even if only to slow down without changing direction). Agreement is less uniform regarding the snowplow turn.

Those against the snowplow turn argue that bad habits are formed and will have to be unlearned if the skier is to progress. So why teach it in the first place? Those in favor of the snowplow turn

92

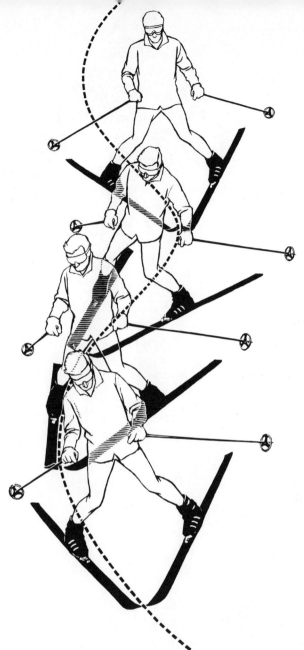

feel that the turn's value is in inspiring confidence in the new skier and letting him come down a gentle slope in control. Everyone admits that excessive snowplowing can form bad habits, and therefore beginners should be urged out of the phase as fast as possible. I agree completely—there is no reason for anyone (except for rare cases) to use snowplow turns after the first three or four days of skiing.

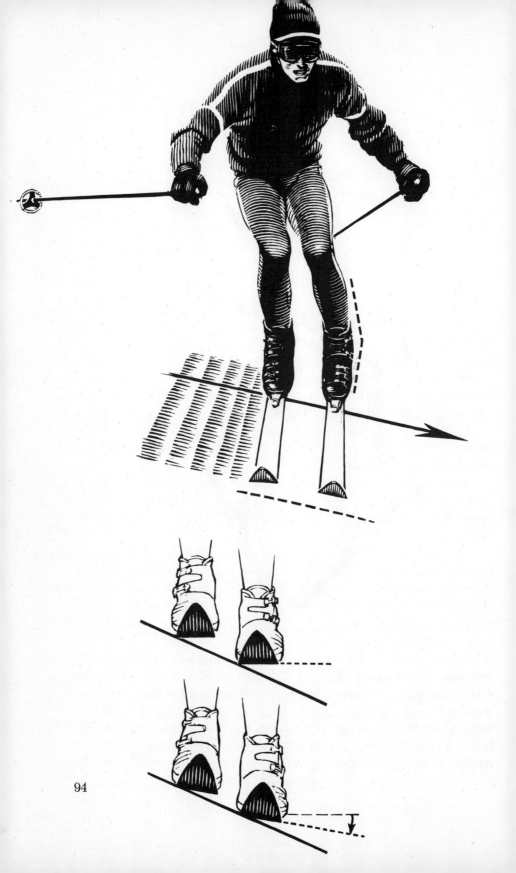

The Skill
of Sideslipping

Once I heard a beginner speak of there being two kinds of skiers. He said, "There are grinders and there are swishers, and I'm tired of grinding my way down. I want to learn to go swish-swish-swish, like the better skiers." He was talking about the differences between the slow turns which many learners use—where the strength of the legs forces and steers the skis around—and the smooth, graceful turns, called christies, which experts use to make their skis skid around effortlessly. That skidding action is known technically as sideslipping.

It requires finesse rather than strength. Since more than three-quarters of a christie involves sideslipping, you can see why it is important to master this skill. It's all a matter of controlling the edges of your skis.

In the large drawing I am practicing sideslipping. I am not turning, but rather allowing myself to slip sideways down the hill. Actually I am moving laterally down the fall line. The small sketches show how I move my knees and ankles away from the hill to decrease the angle the soles of my skis make with the snow. In the upper sketch my skis are edged and I travel in the direction the skis point. But, in the lower one, where I have released my edges, I skid sidways. This is where the finesse comes in. I must not release the edges too much, or I will fall over sideways, downhill. And if I don't release them enough, I won't be able to let my skis sideslip. Most skiers must practice sideslipping—in each direction—for ten hours or more during a period of several days before being real masters of this very necessary skill.

The Uphill Christie

There is no handier maneuver for all skiers than the uphill christie. What is it? Basically, a skidded turn into the hill, variously called a christie into the hill or a christie away from the fall line. It's used as an easy way to avoid obstacles and to slow down, even to the point of coming to a stop. Can you imagine just how much confidence you'll have once you know how to perform this simple maneuver?

Learn it this way. Traverse a smooth-packed slope, preferably one which is pitched twenty degrees or more. As you traverse the slope, move your hips forward to apply definite pressure to the front of each foot. Maintain this position and very gradually move your knees and ankles away from the hill to release the grip of the edges. What happens? You turn *into* the hill—that's what happens—because the extra pressure on the front edges allowed them to hold their grip while the decreased grip on the back edges allowed gravity to pull the heels of the skis downhill.

When you first learn the uphill christie, it's important to let your skis do the turning for you. You must not try to turn or twist the skis with leg or hip power. Instead, you learn to set up the conditions for turning, so the turn can take place on its own: namely, by increased forward lean and decreased angle of edging. Again, don't try to force your skis to turn by twisting your shoulder or jerking hips, legs or feet. Uphill christies take practice because they require finesse rather than strength. It takes time to learn to feel your way around by subtly increasing or decreasing the amount of forward leverage and the amount of edging.

Once you have learned the basics of the uphill christie, it's always possible to turn into the hill and come to a stop—provided you are headed on a traverse and not straight down the fall line. There's another benefit, too: After you have perfected this maneuver, you no longer need to resort to the snowplow to break your speed. The only exception is when schussing the fall line. Another plus connected with the maneuver: Henceforth, any time you start downhill, you know you can always complete a turn because in reality, an uphill christie is nothing but the last half of a parallel downhill christie. Once learned, you can add the polishing ingredients of heel pushing (page 113) and carving (page 145).

The Stem Christie

The stem christie is a ski-school maneuver and it should be abandoned before the stemming movements become a habit almost impossible to correct.

A stem is a movement accomplished by using one leg and foot to separate the tails of the skis. A snowplow is sometimes called a double stem and a stem is sometimes called a half snowplow. In the illustration, you see me traversing a smooth-packed hill. Uphill is to my right. Note that my skis are parallel, my legs comfortably apart, and my body centered and squared directly over my skis. In the second illustration (right to left), I have started to stem. The lower ski (my left) remains edged and on its traversing course. I have picked up the heel of my uphill ski and moved it away from the lower one in the classic uphill stemming manner. Note that I have brought forward my lower pole. The stemming action turns my uphill ski toward the fall line, and then into it. The third figure in the sequence shows me at the moment I'm about to jab my pole into the snow. The moment it is in the snow, I shift my weight to my stemmed ski and move my body by force around the heel of that ski.

In the final figure, I have crossed the fall line. Note that I have now brought the inside ski of my turn alongside of and parallel to the outside ski of the turn. The stemming action is over and the christie or skidding phase has begun. From here on, I merely sideslip around the rest of the turn as if I were making an uphill christie. On page 110, I explained how to move your weight and adjust the angles your edges make in the snow to control the skidding action.

The stem christie must be performed with enough speed to

allow the skis to skid easily—that's between 10 and 15 miles per hour. There's no question about it—skiing becomes really fun once you learn to stem christie—so much fun that too often you forget that this is only part of the way to great skiing. Discard it quickly, and move on to parallel.

5 | KEYS TO PARALLEL

It's NOT VERY LIKELY that anyone who has skied for a day or two does not know what a christie is. But just in case there's someone who doesn't, it's a skidded turn or a controlled slip. Before getting into the details, let me explain the concept loosely like this: When you are skiing down a mountain and you want to change direction by using a christie, the first trick is to alter the angle of your skis to your original direction—enough so that a skid results. The next trick is to control that skid. Of course, you know that to make a christie isn't all that easy; in fact, the technical literature of skiing is filled with many elaborate and confusing technical explanations.

Part of the reason for the confusion is that there are so many different kinds of christies. There is the stem christie, in which you change the angle to your original direction by moving just one ski at a time. But I don't believe it's necessary to explain this turn here— read about it in the previous chapter. I believe that stem christies are just a learner's step toward making parallel turns, so I don't devote much attention to them. If you practice stemming too much, you will get into the habit of moving one ski at a time to such an extent that you may never completely rid yourself of the stem.

Parallel christies are really easy to do and many of them are far less complicated than the stem, believe it or not. The simple fact is that in parallel christies both skis do the same thing at the same time —and both your feet must turn at the same time. Keep in mind,

101

though, that this does not mean your feet and skis have to look as though glued together. When learning, there is nothing wrong with making parallel christies with the feet held apart approximately the width of your hips. After all that is a very steady stance, and balance is the most important thing to preserve at all times in skiing.

In an earlier chapter I said that skiing was fun to learn right from the start, and that it became even more fun as you improved. Well, if you have yet to make your first parallel christie, you can expect to be more amazed than you imagined you could be once you master the art. Being able to ski parallel allows you to slither through moguls, to carve on ice, and to float your way down through waist-deep powder, linking together an endless series of thrilling turns with which you can control your speed.

I thought it might interest you to know something about the word "christie." It really is a shortened version of the word Christiania, the old name for Oslo, the capital of Norway. About one hundred years ago, ski jumpers from that city devised a way to skid themselves to a stop after making one of their crowd-pleasing leaps. This skidded stop became modified into a skidded turn and, though the way it's done now is greatly modified and improved, the name survives.

So much for history. Now for the details on turning. Recall that I mentioned the first trick about parallel christies—turning your skis at an angle to their original direction. Of course you know that your skis are long and they resist turning. So to make the task possible, any time you want to make a parallel christie, you must first unweight them. Then, during the brief moment when they are not pressing against the snow, you must angle them slightly to the original direction. At the same time, roll the skis somewhat so that they will rest on those edges which will become your skidding edges. This chapter will show and explain these three facets, or keys to parallel christies, in detail.

This chapter will also show you how to keep your skid going, and how to control it. Perhaps you never realized it before, but controlling a skid is nothing more or less than making a christie into the hill, which was explained in the last chapter.

Is there anything complicated to understand about this analysis of the parallel christies? Everything else about this amazing turn becomes an embellishment. Of course, you will want to learn these embellishments to polish your skill and develop your true athletic potential. I am referring to things like planting the pole, shifting your weight, and heel pushing. All of these are included in this chapter. But remember this—even though you may understand these keys to christies, practice is needed to unlock the door to success. You can't really learn to ski from a book only, unless you put into practice what you read. The best thing is to get out there on those slopes and ski.

Unweighting:
The First Key

Basically, skis want to go in a straight line on the snow. They are five to seven feet long, have a straight groove down the middle and steel edges that grip the snow. This gives them a kind of "one-track mind." Therefore, for most turns—especially the christies—you have to get your weight off the skis so they lose their tight grip and can be steered into a new direction. This lightening of the skis is called unweighting.

I am doing a parallel christie in this illustration, using pronounced up-unweighting. If you are a beginner, you won't be doing this advanced sort of turn right away, not with long skis anyway, though your instructor might let you try it with short (four foot) ones. As illustrated, first I crouch down and set my edges to get ready to rebound upward. Then I spring up by quickly straightening my legs. This sudden "up" motion results in an unweighting of my skis—sometimes lifting them from the snow. Once the skis are unweighted like this, I can turn them easily.

In most situations a moderate, but fast "up" motion with the skis remaining on the snow allows enough time to start a parallel christie. Note that in the second picture my knees are still slightly bent and my upper body is inclined somewhat forward. I never straighten up all the way because the amount of unweighting depends less on the amount of "up" than it does on the speed of execution. A small but quick, explosive movement is what you should work for.

Another way to unweight is by a downward movement, done correctly by quickly pushing the knees forward and simultaneously

dropping the hips. Though this method gets your weight off the skis for only a fraction of a second, it's long enough for them to loosen their grip so your turning power will take effect. Instructors differ in the emphasis they give to up- or down-unweighting in teaching people to ski. When I analyze films of myself, in a slalom course, for instance, I see that I spring up when I've the time to, and drop down when time is short.

There are times when you need hardly unweight at all, such as on icy snow where your skis can slip around easily, or on moguls, which make your skis easy to swivel because of their shape. In these two situations, you will want to keep your skis down on the snow as much as possible to remain in control and you will have to concentrate to suppress any excess unweighting movements. On the other hand, in deep snow, you will have to work to exaggerate the amount of unweighting.

Turning Power:
The Second Key

There are several ways to apply turning power to your unweighted skis. A popular way is to quickly shift weight to the outside or "turning" ski, as you do for the snowplow turn and the stem turn. Another way, stemming, is to push one foot laterally to the outside of the turn, while using the front of the ski as a movable pivot. A variation of this is to thrust aside the heels of both skis, and that's called heel pushing. It is also possible to swivel both ends of the skis around their middles merely by twisting or rotating the feet and knees in the desired direction. It's also possible to use your arms, shoulders, and torso as a source of rotary power, though that complicates matters.

My preference is using a combination of movements called anticipation. First, as I bring one christie to a definite set of the edges, I lightly twist my upper body in the direction in which I intend to turn. Then, during the brief period that my skis have been unweighted, I twist or crank my knees and feet around in the direction in which my upper body has already begun to move. In this way my upper body never gets behind my feet, and keeping my balance and control over my skis becomes an easy matter. A careful study of the accompanying illustration will perhaps tell you more about this most efficient kind of turning power than words could ever explain.

Edge Change:
The Third Key

When you schuss straight down, your skis rest flat on their running surfaces. When you traverse across the hill, however, each ski should rest on its uphill edge. Let me clarify: Going across with the hill to your left, your skis should rest on their left, or uphill, edges. (In France we call those edges *les carres amont.*) When you make a turn and traverse in the opposite direction, with the hill to your right, the skis rest upon the right edges—again, those on the uphill side. But remember, the uphill side is now to your right.

During the turn, a changing of the edges has had to take place. In the illustration, I show how I change edges by using a banking action. Just like riding a bicycle, I lean my body into the turn. The leaning action causes my skis to roll from one set of edges to the other set. You see me during the half second or less which it takes to change the edges during a normal parallel christie. In the first figure, my skis are on their uphill edges. By visualizing how my body has moved from that position into the second, you'll see the banking action. I actually lean sideways—away from the hill and down toward the valley—just enough to make the skis roll from their uphill edges, flatten on the snow, and then on over to a new set of edges. My ski pole gives a moment's support and prevents me from banking too much. You must change edges with every christie you make.

Banking to change edges is fine for long christies, because the upper body has time to move from side to side. But the closer together and faster I link my turns, the less banking I use. Then I merely change edges by shifting my knees from side to side, angulating first one way, then the other. (See traversing, page 87.)

109

Weight Shifting and Lead Change: Skills for Parallel

In this illustration I am making a christie to my left. In the first figure, my skis are resting on their right edges. After my turn has been completed (last figure) they are resting on their left edges. Follow me through as I change edges and shift my weight from one ski to the other. In Figure 1, I've just ended one turn and I've already begun to shift my weight from the lower ski to the upper one. I plant my ski pole to trigger a christie to my left. In Figure 2, the edge change and weight shift have clearly begun. Note how I've moved my body downhill, leaning slightly into my turn. I've also moved my knees toward the center of the turn, picking up my lower ski as I did so, to make sure that my weight is shifted to what is now the outside ski of my christie. You can see how these movements placed my skis flat to the slope. As an instructor would say, I have banked into my turn to release my edges. Once the skis are flat on the snow like this they skid easily, and I turn myself into the position you see in Figure 3. At this point, I have continued to bank with my body and knees to roll my outside ski (the right one) so it now rests on its new edge. At this point all my weight still rests on that outside ski, helping it to carve its way around. Now, the most difficult part of the turn is over. From here on, I have only to control the skidding action and let the skis skid as much or as little as I want as in an uphill christie. In Figure 4, I have returned my inside ski to the snow for better balance and control. You can almost see the entire bottom surface of my skis because I have allowed the tails to skid around quite far to complete this christie. I am now ready to make a christie to my right.

There is something else that takes place during every christie, though I don't like to dwell too much on this aspect because it usually happens automatically. That's lead change: During a christie the inside foot and ski must gradually move ahead—at least by the time the first half of the turn has been completed. If this does not happen, then of course you will consciously move your inside foot ahead. But when that's the case, you are doing something else wrong. In that event it is best to have your technique checked out by a competent instructor.

Heel Push:
Another Skill for Parallel

Since I hung up my racing skis, I've found a lot of pleasure in our sport and learned a lot more about it, too. When I stop to think, I realize I was lucky I could learn to ski without having to think too much about how to do it. I gave my entire concentration to the task of winning. Now I like to watch people learning to ski and I try to help them. I once saw a man trying to teach his girl to ski on a hill that was too steep for her. She was scared, and, of course, when one is tense, one loses confidence. This man would call to her, "Turn, honey." She wouldn't and he became irritated, calling her dumb.

Well, as all skiers know, turning is not always that simple. I still work on my christies, even today, and one of the skills I work on is called heel pushing. In the illustration, I am almost halfway through a parallel christie to my left. My skis are resting slightly on their inside edges, and I am skidding or sideslipping around. Suddenly, there's an approaching obstacle and I must make a much tighter turn to avoid it. To do this I heel push. Compare the two figures at left, and you can see that I have pushed my heels down the hill, pivoting them around the tips of my skis. To push the heels this way, I first bend my lower ankle away from the turn ever so slightly—my right ankle for this turn. Then I lower my hips quickly by bending at the knees, and, at the same time, push my heels out from under me. Not too far, though! I don't want snow in the back pocket. When I want the skis to stop skidding, I roll my ankle inward again to make the inside edge of the ski grip the snow firmly.

The upper ski also must be able to skid. I control its edge by moving my knee away from the turn. The movements are subtle. Practice a lot, and have an instructor supervise your practice.

Pole Planting:
An Aid to Parallel

If you plan to ski fast and on the steep slopes (who doesn't?) you must master pole planting.

To make your poles work for you, they must be the right length. See page 51 if you are not sure what this is. Remember it's better to have poles an inch or two shorter—ones that are too long will throw you on your *derrière*.

Think of pole planting as a commitment to turn. You spot the place you want to make your christie. You prepare, and, when you reach the spot, the pole closest to the center of your turn is planted hard. *Pow!* You unweight, change edges, and are off in a new direction almost before you know it—if you do it right.

Make it a habit from the very beginning to use your whole arm to make the pole reach the spot. Don't reach with only the tip of the pole by bending your wrist this way and that. It will rob your pole plant of much of its effectiveness if your hand is out of line with your forearm.

In the illustration, you can see just how effective the pole plant can be. I am on a steep slope. On the left, I have firmly gripped the snow with my edges and just planted the pole. In the middle drawing, the pole plant is beginning to take effect. I begin to rise to unweight (you can see this by looking at my legs). I absorb part of the energy of the pole plant with my shoulders and I rotate them in the direction of the turn. In the illustration on the right, I am bracing hard against the pole and my skis come off the snow. It is now easy to change edges and complete my turn.

Pole planting is not hard to do, but it is difficult to perfect. But perfect it you must if you want to turn.

115

6

TRACKS TO SUCCESS— BALANCE AND CONFIDENCE MAKE THE DIFFERENCE

MANY SKIERS can make stem christies—and even parallel christies—but they ski like scared chickens, darting from one panicky turn to another. Their movements are stiff, jerky, and even uncertain. They lack rhythm and grace. And often all that is really wrong with their skiing is that they lack confidence. They are determined, often trying to make a sort of sequence of maneuvers fit the hill. And that is impossible to do. You must learn to feel your way down a mountain, never brutalizing the slope, but rather making it a willing partner. This takes confidence, for if you show any signs of fear, you'll lose your capacity to think and feel your maneuvers.

Practice, and lots of it, is in order, so that you will be able to do the basic maneuvers on strange slopes, with changing snow and changing terrain. You must be able to take all those changes in stride—don't avoid them; instead, look for places to practice going fast—skiing through hollows, skiing over bumps and the like. Sometimes, in ski school, the instructor becomes so anxious trying to teach you maneuvers that he forgets to give you the experiences which develop rhythm, grace, and confidence—things that make skiing exciting and easy.

In this chapter you'll find a lot of advice which will help you ski like a spirit in the wind—in other words, with freedom. You'll be able to improvise, to ski the way you feel instead of like a mechanical robot.

117

The Steady Stance

Skiing is a game of balance. It's my belief that anyone who can walk, run, and especially dance, has enough natural sense of balance to become a good skier. But there are certain things you can learn to make it easier to stay in balance. The most important one is knowing the correct way to stand on your skis.

In the illustration, see how I am in a sort of slump. My knees are pushed forward so that I have a flexible bend at the ankles and knees. More important, my shoulders are slightly rounded and I have a slight bend at the waist. This overall position makes it easy for me to keep my weight resting on the soles of my feet, with most of it pressing against the ball of each foot—as it should be most of the time. By keeping my shoulders forward the way I do—never letting them go further back than to where the illustration shows—I make sure that I will never be knocked over backward, the way most learners fall. I may bend further forward at the waist, but not further backward, not even to the point where I would be standing with my back almost upright.

Use a Wide Stance
for Balance

Here's a skiing tip that I learned from M. Honoré Bonnet, the coach of the French ski team. I was falling during races because I was losing my balance, and he felt the reason for this was that I was holding my feet together. That, he said, interfered with the natural independent working of the legs. The advice he gave me was simple —ski with your feet apart.

I got into the feet-together habit, and it was hard to overcome. I was trying to race and look like a stylist. But once I really understood this, I had no trouble in doing the right thing. Stand on your two feet, Jean-Claude, I said, and race. Forget about style. I now advise you to do the same.

I found the best stance for me was with my feet six to eight inches apart—seldom any closer than that, but often wider, as you can see by the illustration. Of course, if I want to ski with a flashy style when skiing for pleasure, I can almost glue my boots together, but I find that I lose freedom to change direction quickly and to maneuver in difficult passages. What's more, I really have to concentrate on keeping my balance.

Because of my experiences, I suggest you learn to ski with your feet comfortably apart. When you feel at ease on the snow, then is the time to concentrate on looking stylish.

Skating for Balance
and Confidence

I've won more than a few races by aggressively skating between gates to accelerate and get in the best position for the next turn. But, skating is not just for competitors—it can help give your skiing a racer's confidence. Furthermore, a few fast skating steps at the start of your skiing day will warm you up and put you in a "forceful" frame of mind—important, if your skiing is to improve.

As you practice skating you will build your sense of balance and what we call *l'indépendance des jambes* (independence of the legs). This is the ability to ski on one leg independently of the other, an important skill in modern skiing. You also learn edge control and build strength in the muscles that control edging (ankles, knees, and hips).

Here's how to skate on skis. As you see in the sequence illustrations, I push off from the edged back ski, transfer my weight to the other ski, which I have already thrust out at an angle. But first, my upper body and hips twist and lean in the direction of the thrusting ski. Notice that after the push-off from the back ski, I quickly bring it alongside the forward ski, lifting its tip off the snow so it doesn't catch. All of my weight is now on the forward or sliding ski. The other ski remains in the air but comes more or less parallel to the sliding ski, as I start to lean and twist my body to the opposite side. Then I angle out the new thrusting ski and push off with the skating foot. What more can I tell you? It's skating, such as on ice skates—that's all.

I do have a few more suggestions: When first learning, don't use your poles—they may trip you. Later, learn to hold them more

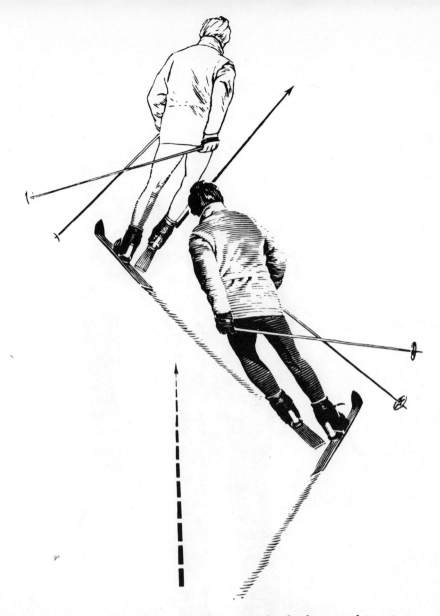

or less parallel to the slope. To edge your back ski so it bites into the snow and gives you a platform to push off from, roll your ankle and knee inward just before the push-off. Also be sure that you bend your leg and lower your hips so that you can push off with enthusiasm and get a nice long glide on the front foot.

After you can skate going straight ahead, try turning to one side as you move—it's a good way to change direction. Then try skating when you are going down a moderate slope and also try the skating turn. *Magnifique!* You're on your way to turning like a racer.

Develop Confidence

For me, downhill racing was the toughest of the three disciplines of Alpine skiing to conquer. I had naturally quick reflexes and, once I perfected my techniques, slalom races were the easiest to win. And, because I worked hard to develop my strength, I was able to triumph in giant slalom events. But developing my self-confidence was what finally enabled me to win an Olympic gold medal in the downhill.

You, too, must become confident before you will enjoy the thrills of skiing. In the illustration, I've been launched into the air and I have just extended my legs to prepare for landing. The timing of my movements must be exact. If I lose my nerve, even for a split second, I would be off and I could take a bad fall. Believe me, I had to build up my confidence before I could sail off a bump at 100 kilometers (62.5 miles) an hour!

It is a normal part of skiing for everyone, beginner or expert, to be accidentally launched into the air. To learn to enjoy the thrill without losing nerve, take time to practice jumping. Beginners should learn to hop while sliding at 5 miles an hour. Intermediates should be able to sail comfortably off a one-foot high bump, going 10 miles an hour, and travel in the air for a ski length or two. Advanced skiers should be able to do much more than that!

Gradually build up your confidence, never going off bumps which would be dangerous for a skier of your ability. Practice regularly, always daring yourself by going just a bit faster, higher, and farther than the last time. Then, when you accidentally become airborne, you will not lose your nerve. Instead, you will enjoy the thrills more than ever.

Teach Yourself to Recover

Trouble can come in many forms—icy patches, unexpected changes in the steepness of the slope, bumps, ruts, and lots of other things. Your own mistakes can get you into trouble. Of course, the more alert you are the less likely you are to get into trouble. But don't bet on it. *Learn* to make a recovery.

The important thing is to stay cool. Almost always there's more time than you think. I know this because I have made lots of recoveries in slalom where there is supposed to be no time between turns. Many people have said to me, "Jean-Claude, those are wild recoveries you make," but I don't think they really understand. A recovery isn't a very spectacular thing, but some of the turns that followed my recoveries may have been a bit wild. However, I could make them only because I was secure again, turning from a very solid stance.

You see me here when I was crossing some very bad ruts at high speed, prior to making a turn to the right. A moment before, I had been standing up quite straight to see what was ahead and I was almost knocked off-balance. Just in the nick of time I recovered by doing several things simultaneously. First, I dropped my hips very low (lowered my center of gravity), put my feet farther apart, and spread my arms a bit to make sure of my stability. I pushed my left (uphill) ski ahead a bit so that a bump couldn't affect both legs at the same time. And I squared my stance to make sure I had completely recovered my balance. I made my turn a fraction late, but better a late turn than a fall. You can learn to make recoveries, too. And since you have no gates to make, you have even more time in which to regain control.

Ski Tall,
Ski Small,
and Adapt to Terrain

Sometimes I ski standing tall. Other times I crouch low. It's not because of some whim, but because my position varies as the terrain does.

Here you see me demonstrating the extremes of both positions. The illustrations were made from photos taken during my medal-winning races at the XII Winter Olympics. To become a good skier, learn to make use of those extremes in the way you stand on your skis. If the terrain is smooth, stand tall and let the springiness which the knees and ankles provide go to work for you, absorbing the minor bumps and hollows which are always present. If the terrain is rough, let your legs buckle up deeply underneath you whenever you feel that the bumps want to compress you. Even many good skiers won't let their bodies fold up as much as I do, and there are plenty of times they should.

Your body must never become frozen into a tall or a small position. It must vary all the time, flexing up and down so that your skis and your head get as smooth a ride as possible.

Crossing from
Flat Slope to Steep

If you are skiing on a relatively flat slope and come to a steeper one, you must learn to anticipate the sudden acceleration you'll get. You do this by leaning forward before you get to the steeper pitch, no later than the time that your feet reach the crest of the drop-off. Keep your hands in front of your hips (as you see in the illustration) which will help you keep your weight forward. If you don't anticipate in this way, your skis will go scooting out in front of you with their new-found acceleration and you will fall backward on your *derrière*.

A similar situation arises when you go from slower snow to faster snow—such as from unpacked to packed, or from good snow to ice. Again you must anticipate your scooting skis and lean forward before you reach the faster snow.

After you have completed the transition onto the steeper or faster slope, you can resume your original upright balanced position.

A

A

B

B

Crossing from
Steep Slope to Flat

In my downhill racing days, I'd often reach speeds of 80 miles per hour or more. At speeds like that you have to anticipate transitions in terrain if you want to stay in one piece. But it's important for you, even at 8 miles per hour, to look ahead and see what's coming up. Bumps, hollows, icy spots, soft spots—all await the unwary. One of the terrain changes that used to give me trouble was the transition from a steep slope to a flat. As your skis go through this, it feels like your body is being compressed and that you are about to be pitched forward onto your face. And believe me, that's just what can happen unless you're ready.

When you are skiing from steep to flat, you must anticipate the change. Your momentum will flatten you out; your skis will slow down more than you think. Get ready by leaning back a bit just before the skis go through the change. Absorb the forward and downward forces by bending at your ankles, knees, and waist. Compress downward, but don't collapse. This rapid slowing also occurs when you go from packed slopes to deep, loose powder. Again, anticipate the change.

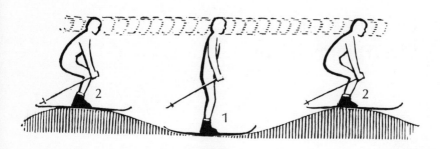

How to Negotiate the Bumps

When you began skiing, you probably spent all of your time on a smooth beginners' slope. That was good—no bumps to throw you, so you could develop a good balance gradually. However, away from the golf-course slopes it's a different story—most hills have bumps. These may be small and frequent, giving a "washboard" ride that rattles your teeth. Or there can be bigger, even head-high moguls that give you a roller-coaster effect and make you miserable until you learn to handle them. Then they are fun and exciting.

Here I am going through a series of moguls. See how my legs are extended in the hollow between the moguls and retracted on the crests. Also, my skis follow the bumpy contour of the terrain, but my head, shoulders, and neck stay on a straight line moving down the slope. I have erased the effect the moguls would have on me if I remained stiff-legged. In France, we call this *avalement* (a-val-MAH), which means swallowing—you swallow the mogul.

Let's look at it in steps: You approach a bump in normal, erect stance. Don't bend forward from the waist before you get to it. As your skis start climbing up the bump let your legs retract under your body and start leaning forward from the waist. When you are at the crest you should be in a crouched position, arms low and in front of your body. When you pass the crest, consciously extend your legs back down into the hollow to keep your skis firmly on the snow and to get control you wouldn't have if they were in space. At the bottom of the hollow, you should again have an extended, almost erect stance. As the next bump comes along, let your "landing gear retract" at the crest and let down on the other side. Practice will give you the right timing.

135

7 PUTTING IT ALL TOGETHER

WHAT A SPORT, this skiing thing! Sometimes you have great days, feeling like the King of the Mountain. Other times, it's just not your day. Nothing seems to go right. You fall, keep catching edges, and have to fight the mountain.

What makes the difference? Often, it's a change in snow conditions. Perhaps you learned to ski on very hard snow. Then, suddenly, you are faced with a few inches of powder or soft pack. Now, your skis don't skid as easily because edge control is more subtle. Or perhaps, after skiing on soft snow, where you've adapted by using more up motion to unweight and kept your weight evenly distributed on both skis, you'll come across that hard stuff which skiers in New England call "loud powder." On that kind of surface, it may be necessary to definitely carry much more weight on your lower ski. That means you must shift your weight from turn to turn.

Frustrating it can be. But how much better it is if you think of changing snow as a fascinating challenge. You can overcome the conditions. Sometimes your equipment is not suitable for the snow or the speeds at which you are trying to ski. Other times it may be that your boots no longer give enough support. Or your steel edges need attention. Keep your eyes and ears open; ask questions; take lessons—and remember—you can overcome. Believe me, there is no snow condition which you cannot ski—and have fun.

It does take practice, time, and lots of experience. Gradually

you'll develop what I like to call *"l'intelligence des pieds"*—the intelligence of the feet. After a while your feet and legs feel everything that goes on between snow and skis, and almost miraculously they will compensate for changes in snow, speed, and terrain automatically. You then become free to enjoy the sport, to savor every thrilling moment, and to improvise your way down the mountain. It's almost like finally having your own wings, to soar and swoop with the freedom of a bird. Believe me, it's worth striving for. As I said in the very beginning of this book, skiing is amazing. There is no end to the thrills and fun in store for you.

In this concluding chapter, you'll find a number of hints and maneuvers to help you fully develop your own wings. I hope you will learn them, put everything together, then take off down the mountain skiing with great fun, control, and style—your own very style. Good luck and good skiing!

Plan Your Line

Skiing is second nature to me. I no longer think about the position of my arms legs, and body, but I do think about the course ahead of me. I had to train myself to concentrate on that, and I think it is an important thing for all skiers, from beginners to Olympic champions, to learn.

In the illustration I am about to go into a turn. But note where I am looking—not where I am, but where I will be. I have trained myself to look at least two turns ahead. So should you.

When making a turn, you will not know exactly how much or where to turn if you look only at your feet or ski tips. Nor will you be able to anticipate bumps, ruts, ice, and changes in pitch. So it will be impossible for you to ski smoothly and rhythmically.

You must train yourself to look where you will be so that, like a racer, you can plan your line. As soon as you spot a good place to turn, ski toward it, but immediately start looking for the next good one so that you know how much to turn to get there. Looking ahead is the only way to determine this. And, forcing yourself to concentrate is the only way to develop the look-ahead habit.

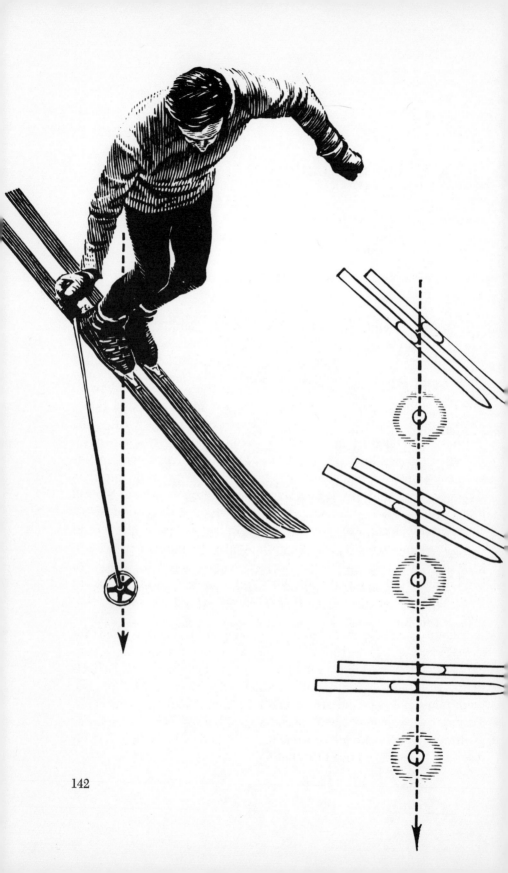

Where to Plant
Your Pole

When you start to perfect your christies, it's time to learn to use your ski pole as a sort of axis for each turn. Think of it this way: The pole stuck in the snow is the axle; your arm is the spoke; and you and your skis are out on the rim. Part of how and where you plant your pole is personal preference, but the illustration shows a rule that applies to everyone. Plant your pole at such a point that a line joining it to about the center of your skis would constitute the fall line. The illustration explains it better. The line running down the hill from my feet is the fall line. I've planted my pole on this imaginary line, approximately an arm's length away from my feet. (The top diagram shows my position for the christie seen in the full illustration). The line running through my foot at the center of the ski is the fall line and the circle is where I plant my pole. The second diagram shows my skis pointing more across the hill as I prepare to plant my pole. So, by the rule, the pole is again planted right down the fall line from my foot. The third diagram shows where I would plant it if I were heading straight across the hill during a stop christie.

Plant your pole in different ways, depending on the need—for example, as an aid to the up movement in up-unweighting. Or to get acceleration in doing a racing turn. Or you can place the pole off to the side more to assist with a quick edge change. Skillful pole plant takes practice, and also strength in arms, shoulders, and chest. To improve, you may need special strengthening exercises such as push-ups. Get the advice of someone who knows his skiing and ski teaching to see if you need this help.

Finishing the Turn —
Carving

There's no single turn for every situation in skiing. The technique I'm using here—carving—holds your speed through a turn. It's a favorite with racers because it minimizes sideslipping and drifting and lets you hold your line and speed as you come around.

In the illustration, note how I have raised my right knee and foot so that only a slight amount of weight rests on the front part of the right ski. That ski—the one on the inside of the christie—held momentarily in the position shown, acts as a stabilizer for my balance. Here I am putting the outside ski (my left one) to work. By placing most of my weight on that ski, I cause it to bend deeply and I force its edge to bite the snow firmly. As a consequence, the ski and I turn more sharply. If I start to turn too sharply, I need only press my inside ski back to the snow to equalize my weight over each ski. Then neither one will bend as much as the outside one did before, and I'll make a longer turn. Shifting weight back and forth between the skis can be done less obviously than I demonstrate here. Learn to feel how your skis respond to your shifts of weight and work them accordingly.

Practice Slalom
to Gain Confidence

I'm sure you've had this experience: you traverse a slope full of mean-looking bumps looking for a place to turn. Suddenly you notice a likely looking spot. You set your edges, plant your pole, get all set for a precision turn, and *wham!* You run into the bumps just past the spot you had picked.

Of course you turned late, but knowing that doesn't cure your problem. While there are many reasons for this to happen, most likely you were thinking too much about the details of how to make a turn instead of concentrating on the turn itself. The best way to break this habit is to practice some slalom.

You say you're no racer, that slalom isn't for you? But it is. Slalom was invented to simulate skiing through the woods, to make skiers demonstrate that they had 100 per cent control over their skis by being able to turn where the course setter decides they should. He does this by setting gates. Each gate consists of two poles set some distance apart and the skier skis between the poles. In this fashion he goes from gate to gate until he reaches the end. Slalom can be as easy or as difficult as necessary.

Try slalom as soon as you have learned to turn—even with simple snowplow turns. You don't need regular slalom gates—stick some branches into the snow about fifteen to twenty feet apart on an easy slope (*see illustration*), and concentrate on skiing between them. Turn as close as possible to the inner branch and force yourself to look ahead at the gate beyond the one you are going through. If it becomes too easy, close up the gates or go to a more difficult slope. Keep it up as you progress. Then when you ski on an open

146

slope you will be able to turn almost where ever you want. You won't worry about bumps. If slalom teaches you anything it is that you must find a way to cope with terrain as it is. This is the best discipline to stop you from looking for the easy way out on a hard slope.

Ski the Powder

Since my life is no longer dominated by ski racing, I have had time to learn about pleasure skiing—and it's fun! Not that I begrudge my years of racing, because I seldom had the time to be bored. But, I must admit, I never really learned to have fun on the slopes, nor did I have much chance to ski in deep snow—really deep powder where you may never see your skis all day long. Now, deep-snow skiing holds the greatest excitement for me. You must try it. You hear only the softest sound from your skis as they slip through the snow. On hard snow, when you make a mistake—catch an edge for instance—it will only distract your ski for a moment or two. Then you can pull it back into line. But, in deep powder, a mistake can cause you to catch your whole ski, and the pressure of the snow makes it hard to pull it back into line. As a result, you often end up—well, upended!

Don't let this scare you away from the powder. To handle it correctly, first learn to stand a new way on your skis—not the same as for packed snow. Learn to keep your weight distributed evenly on your feet. If your bindings are mounted too far forward or if the fronts of your skis are too stiff, it may be necessary to sit back slightly so that your weight presses back on your heels. At first, learn to schuss a gentle powder slope. Keep your weight slightly more on your heels. This is different from schussing on hardpack, where you must keep slightly more weight on the fronts of the skis. If there are no gentle powder slopes around, learn to traverse steep ones. Remember—keep your weight evenly distributed on both skis, not on the lower ski as you do when traversing hardpack.

Learn
the Geländesprung

Strange how language works. In English you use a German word to describe what I'm doing in the illustration, while in French we use a Norwegian word. Americans says *geländesprung* or "gelandy," and we French say *op-trakken*. No matter what you call it, it is a terrain jump, so-called to distinguish it from the classic prepared ski jump.

Nowadays a terrain jump is usually done for the fun of flying through the air for five, ten, maybe even one hundred feet. However, it wasn't always this way. In the early days of skiing, up to about 1935, for safety's sake skiers had to jump over partially hidden fences, over roofs of Alpine hay huts, off small cliffs, and sometimes even across small streams or gaping crevasses in the glaciers. In those days prepared courses were rare indeed. Now, it's only necessary to make a terrain jump when you are skiing fast and must avoid a big bump. Gelandies are fun, however, because of the confidence you develop knowing you can jump if you have to, and because of the *joie de vivre* that comes from being airborne.

In the illustration, I am jumping through space with my legs partially tucked up underneath me. This ski-tips-down position looks spectacular, but it puts my skis parallel to the slope, ready for a smooth landing. I must emphasize that before my skis touch the ground, I extend my legs. They must be able to bend fully to absorb the shock of landing. The flatter the landing slope, the greater the shock will be.

To learn to gelandy, look for a small bump—about two feet high—which is followed by a landing slope that's smooth for at least

three ski lengths. It should not be pitched at anything less than fifteen degrees. Climb up the slope a short distance and begin to ski down toward the take-off spot. On your first few attempts, don't try to spring off—merely let yourself sail through the air for a ski length or so. The first thing to develop is confidence and balance in the air. Do this by maintaining the same position you had at the moment of take-off. If the landing is quite steep, however, you will have to lean your body forward while airborne so that your skis won't shoot out from under you when you land. Gradually increase your speed and the size of the bump. Before long, you'll add tremendous confidence and aggressiveness to your ability because you'll be able to leap over all kinds of lesser obstacles.

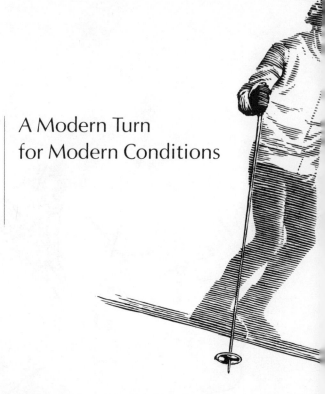

A Modern Turn
for Modern Conditions

For some of you advanced skiers *avalement* is easier to do than to pronounce. As I've said before, it's a French word that means swallowing—and what you do is swallow up the bumps or moguls with your legs. It's hard for many skiers because part of the action is opposite to what they have been practicing for years. For example, you are usually taught to unweight your skis before making a parallel christie by using a rapid, *upward* movement. But for "swallowing" you must unweight by means of a very quick downward motion.

The swift sinking momentarily makes your skis lighter. At that instant, you must twist your knees and feet into the direction of your turn. In the illustration, the turn is downhill to my right.

As in all christies, proper timing is important. Begin *avalement* christies by planting your pole on the crest of the mogul. Immediately follow by dropping your hips so quickly that your skis will unweight the moment your feet arrive at the crest. Then swivel your hips and begin to rise up by partially straightening the legs. The rising action forces your skis down to conform to the shape of the mogul. As a result, you make a very swift sure-carving turn

around it. The sense of control is amazing. Master *avalement* and you are on your way to becoming a thoroughly accomplished, expert skier.

GOOD   **BAD**

Check Your Edges
for Holding Power
on Hard Snow and Ice

The illustration shows how my skis hold me into a turn, even on the hard stuff. Part of the reason is that I always see to it that my edges are not merely sharp, but sharp in the right way. The cutaway drawings show the difference between a good and a bad edge. To provide maximum holding power, the bottom of the steel edges must be honed or filed so they are perfectly flush with the plastic surface of the ski sole. If the edges protrude downward from the sole at any point, this protrusion will both slow you down and give trouble during christies. Again, if the edge bottom has been filed so that it is less than flush with the sole, you will have lost a lot of holding power for any kind of snow. You will also lose holding power if the side of the edge is not filed to a right angle with the bottom (*see cutaway of bad edge*).

I'm not a scientist or an engineer, so this is an estimate, but I am sure that if the edge is not flat to the bottom within a degree or two either way, your skis will not perform as well as they are designed to. If the angles are not correct, file them! If you don't know how, have an instructor or ski shop show you.

Sharpness can be gauged by drawing your thumbnail across the edge. If the edge is sharp, it will shave a thin white film off your nail. If it doesn't, don't expect to have skis that hold on hardpack. A sharpening job is in order. Details like these seem small but they make the difference. Don't lose out on great skiing because of laziness.

Skiing on Hard Snow

Though we dream of untracked powder snow, much of the time we must ski on hard and often icy slopes. Packed snow usually gets harder as it is skied on. A thaw followed by a freeze makes for hard, icy snow. As a ski racer, I didn't mind hard snow; in fact, in slalom racing it is ideal because ruts don't develop as fast and every racer has a good, consistent surface to ski on. However, it's a real test of your equipment and technique.

First your edges must be properly sharpened, as I explained on the previous page. If you don't want to do your own sharpening, have it done at a ski shop. Racers use very stiff boots which make an almost rigid lateral connection between the leg and the ski, and this helps them edge into the hard stuff. Your boots needn't be painfully stiff, but they must not be broken down or floppy. The same goes for your skis. If they have lost their liveliness either in a lengthwise or torsional direction, they won't handle hard snow. If your boots rock laterally in the bindings, you'll lose vital control over the sharpest edges. If your skis sideslip when you don't want them to, then inadequate equipment might be part of your problem. Ask an instructor or ski shop to inspect your gear.

If it's adequate, skiing precisely on hard snow should be relatively easy. To traverse, subtly increase the bite of your edges by using angulation—push your knees into the hill while allowing your body to lean away from the hill so that your shoulders become more or less parallel to the slope. Also, keep your skis apart and weighted equally, with your weight pressing down over the whole of each foot, not just the toes or heels, to make the full-bearing length of each edge bite the ice.

Turning on icy snow takes special consideration, too. Look at the carved christie I am starting in the illustration. In the first figure I'm in an angulated position with my skis apart and equally weighted. Next, I twist my feet and legs just enough to sort of sneak my skis into the fall line. I carefully avoid too much turning power —to be sure that the skis will not skid out of my intended track. For the same reason, I use very little up-unweighting. I do not want to turn my skis so much that they enter into an uncontrollable skid. Gentle precision is what to strive for, not brute haste. Once the turn is started, I rely on the built-in turning action of the skis to complete the christie, just putting my skis in position to help them do their work. To do this, my knees must move toward the inside of the turn. Instructors call this *reangulating,* and it helps concentrate most of the weight on the inside edges of the skis. If I find my skis tend to slip out from under me, then I press more on my lower ski, forcing its edge into the snow. If I still cannot hold and control my direction precisely, I know I have pushed the skis to their maximum potential, and I just must learn to enjoy their limitations by sideslipping.

A Turn for Moguls

Moguls can help you to unweight, pivot your skis in the new direction, and make the proper change of edges—things which are the guts of any parallel turn.

Here's how to do this mogul christie. I ride my skis to the mogul and as my tips pass the crest, I plant my pole at the top of the bump, comfortably off to the side. Note the pole placement in the first figure. Also, I've started to anticipate the direction of this approaching right turn by bringing my right shoulder and arm forward while letting my body tip slightly toward the fall line. These movements will make it easier to give turning power to the skis at the brief instant they are balanced on the crest of the mogul, tips and tails ever so slightly off the snow. At this pivot point my skis will swivel easily because only that small area under my feet touches snow. As my feet pass over this point, I quickly move my knees to the inside of the turn, and twist my feet into the desired direction. This forces the skis to pivot, and changes them to the inside edges of the new turn.

The second figure shows that I've lowered my hips to absorb some of the jolt of the bump, and to unweight my skis. Once the skis have turned, I move my hips up and forward, as in the third figure, to cause the skis to regain full contact with the snow. They will skid around easily to complete the christie, and I'll control its radius by the amount of edging and steering I do with my knees and feet—as in any christie into the hill.

Practice this easy christie by stopping on top of a mogul and balancing in the pivot position I described. Plant your pole and support yourself on it. Then, in a smooth sequence, lower your hips,

158

crank your feet and knees around, and tip forward with your upper
body. Push off the pole and—*whoosh*—pivot, down and around you
go.

About Doug Pfeiffer

Doug Pfeiffer began skiing at the age of four on the slopes around his birthplace, Quebec City, Canada. In his late teens he developed an interest in ski racing and managed to place in the first ten to twenty in most Laurentian Zone events. But, because he found racing so limited, his interest changed from competition to teaching which he began doing at Laurentian resorts, including Mont Tremblant and Gray Rocks, and twice passed the Canadian Ski Instructors Alliance examinations as top man of the year.

In 1950, Doug left Canada to join Emile Allais, one of the world's greatest racers and ski teachers, at Squaw Valley, California. While at Squaw, he was certified at the Far West Ski Instructors Association examinations, again as top man, and subsequently served as president of that organization. He later became one of the founders of the Professional Ski Instructors of America and went on to teach, organize ski schools, and coach junior racers—many of whom went on to race in the Olympics.

He obtained his B.A. in education and taught public school in California for three years. In 1963, Doug moved to Colorado to become National Editor of *Skiing* magazine and also headed the ski school at Loveland Basin.

Since 1965, he has been based in New York as Editor-in-Chief of *Skiing,* and travels extensively to keep abreast of the ski instruction scene. He has participated in a series of more than a hundred TV ski shows, done numerous radio broadcasts, and countless public appearances before ski clubs, civic organizations, and both professional and amateur organizations in the ski industry. In the winter of 1970, he appeared on nationwide TV as commentator and consultant for CBS's "The Killy Challenge" series.